TExES 154

English as a Second Language Supplemental

Teacher Certification Exam Guide
By: Sharon Wynne, M.S.

XAMonline, INC.
Boston

To obtain permission(s) to use the material from this work for any purpose including workshops or seminars, please submit a written request to:

XAMonline, Inc.
21 Orient Avenue
Melrose, MA 02176
Toll Free 1-800-509-4128
Email: info@xamonline.com
Web: www.xamonline.com
Fax: 1-617-583-5552

Library of Congress Cataloging-in-Publication Data

Wynne, Sharon A.

TExES English as a Second Language Teacher Certification / Sharon A. Wynne
ISBN 978-1-60787-387-7

1. English as a Second Language (ESL)   2. Study Guides.
3. TExES   4. Teachers' Certification & Licensure   5. Careers

Disclaimer:
The opinions expressed in this publication are solely those of XAMonline and were created independently from the National Education Association, Educational Testing Service, and any State Department of Education, National Evaluation Systems or other testing affiliates.

Between the time of publication and printing, state-specific standards as well as testing formats and website information may produce change that is not included in part or in whole within this product. Sample test questions are developed by XAMonline and reflect similar content to real tests; however, they are not former tests. XAMonline assembles content that aligns with state standards but makes no claims nor guarantees teacher candidates a passing score. Numerical scores are determined by testing companies such as NES or ETS and then are compared with individual state standards. A passing score varies from state to state.

Printed in the United States of America
TExES English as a Second Language (ESL)
ISBN: 978-1-60787-387-7

<u>About XAMonline</u>

Founded in 1996, XAMonline began with a teacher-in-training who was frustrated by the lack of materials available for certification exam preparation. XAMonline has grown from publishing one state-specific guide to offering guides for every state exam in the U.S., as well as the PRAXIS series.

Each study guide offers more than just the competencies and skills required to pass a certification exam. The core text material leads the teacher beyond rote memorization of skills to mastery of the subject matter, a necessary step for effective teaching.

XAMonline's unique publishing model brings currency and innovation to teacher preparation:

- Print-on-demand technology allows for the most up-to-date guides that are first to market when tests change or are updated.
- The highest quality standards are maintained by using seasoned, professional teachers who are experts in their fields to author the guides.
- Each guide includes varied levels of rigor in a comprehensive practice test so that the study experience closely matches the actual in-test experience.
- The content of the guides is relevant and engaging.

At its inception, XAMonline was a forward-thinking company, and we remain committed to bringing new ways of studying and learning to the teaching profession. We choose from a pool of over 1500 certified teachers to review, edit, and write our guides. We partner with technology firms to bring innovation to study habits, offering online test functionality, a personalized flashcard builder, and eBooks that allow teachers-in-training to make personal notes, highlight, and study the material in a variety of ways.

To date, XAMonline has helped nearly 500,000 teachers pass their certification or licensing exams. Our commitment to preparation exceeds the expectation of simply providing the proper material for study; it extends from helping teachers gain mastery of the subject matter and giving them the tools to become the most effective classroom leaders possible to ushering today's students toward a successful future.

Three full Practice Tests

Now with Adaptive Assessments!

Adaptive learning is an educational method which uses computers as interactive teaching devices. Computers adapt the presentation of educational material according to students' learning needs, as indicated by their responses to questions. The technology encompasses aspects derived from various fields of study including computer science, education, and psychology.

In Computer Adaptive Testing (CAT), the test subject is presented with questions that are selected based on their level of difficulty in relation to the presumed skill level of the subject. As the test proceeds, the computer adjusts the subject's score based on their answers, continuously fine-tuning the score by selecting questions from a narrower range of difficulty.

The results are available immediately, the amount of time students spend taking tests decreases, and the tests provided more reliable information about what students know—especially those at the very low and high ends of the spectrum. With Adaptive Assessments, the skills that need more study are immediately pinpointed and reported to the student.

Adaptive assessments provide a unique way to assess your preparation for high stakes exams. The questions are asked at the mid-level of difficulty and then, based on the response, the level of difficulty is either increased or decreased. Thus, the test adapts to the competency level of the learner. This is proven method which is also used by examinations such as SAT and GRE. The Adaptive Assessment Engine used for your online self-assessment is based on a robust adaptive assessment algorithm and has been validated by a large pool of test takers. Use this robust and precise assessment to prepare for your exams.

Our Adaptive Assessments can be accessed here: **xamonline.4dlspace.com/AAE**
You will be presented with a short form to complete for your account registration. You will need an active email address to register.

TABLE OF CONTENTS

DOMAIN I   **LANGUAGE CONCEPTS AND LANGUAGE ACQUISITION** 1

COMPETENCY 1   THE ESL TEACHER UNDERSTANDS FUNDAMENTAL LANGUAGE CONCEPTS AND KNOWS THE STRUCTURE AND CONVENTIONS OF THE ENGLISH LANGUAGE 1

SKILL 1.1   Understand the nature of language and basic concepts of language systems (e.g., phonology, morphology, syntax, lexicon, semantics, discourse, pragmatics) and use this understanding to facilitate student learning in the ESL classroom 1

SKILL 1.2   Know the functions and registers of language (e.g., social versus academic language) in English and use this knowledge to develop and modify instructional materials, deliver instruction, and promote ESL students' English language proficiency 11

SKILL 1.3   Understand the interrelatedness of listening, speaking, reading, and writing and use this understanding to develop ESL students' English language proficiency 13

SKILL 1.4   Know the structure of the English language (e.g., word formation, grammar, sentence structure) and the patterns and conventions of written and spoken English and use this knowledge to model and provide instruction in English 16

COMPETENCY 2   THE ESL TEACHER UNDERSTANDS THE PROCESSES OF FIRST-LANGUAGE (L1) AND SECOND-LANGUAGE (L2) ACQUISITION AND THE INTERRELATEDNESS OF L1 AND L2 DEVELOPMENT 21

SKILL 2.1   Know theories, concepts, and research related to L1 and L2 acquisition 21

SKILL 2.2   Use knowledge of theories, concepts, and research related to L1 and L2 acquisition to select effective, appropriate methods and strategies for promoting students' English language development at various stages 24

SKILL 2.3   Know cognitive processes (e.g., memorization, categorization, generalization, metacognition) involved in synthesizing and internalizing language rules for second-language acquisition 25

SKILL 2.4   Analyze the interrelatedness of first- and second-language acquisition and ways in which L1 may affect development of L2 27

SKILL 2.5   Know common difficulties (e.g., idiomatic expressions; L1 interference in syntax, phonology, and morphology) experienced by ESL students in learning English and effective strategies for helping students overcome those difficulties 29

DOMAIN II   **ESL INSTRUCTION AND ASSESSMENT**..............................31

COMPETENCY 3   THE ESL TEACHER UNDERSTANDS ESL TEACHING METHODS AND USES THIS KNOWLEDGE TO PLAN AND IMPLEMENT EFFECTIVE, DEVELOPMENTALLY APPROPRIATE INSTRUCTION 31

SKILL 3.1   Know applicable Texas Essential Knowledge and Skills (TEKS), especially the English Language Proficiency Standards (ELPS), and know how to design and implement appropriate instruction to address the domains of listening, speaking, reading, and writing 31

SKILL 3.2   Know effective instructional methods and techniques for the ESL classroom, and select and use instructional methods, resources, and materials appropriate for addressing specified instructional goals and promoting learning in students with diverse characteristics and needs 34

SKILL 3.3   Apply knowledge of effective practices, resources, and materials for providing content-based ESL instruction, engaging students in critical thinking, and fostering students' communicative competence 39

SKILL 3.4   Know how to integrate technological tools and resources into the instructional process to facilitate and enhance student learning........41

SKILL 3.5   Apply effective classroom management and teaching strategies for a variety of ESL environments and situations 43

COMPETENCY 4   THE ESL TEACHER UNDERSTANDS HOW TO PROMOTE STUDENTS' COMMUNICATIVE LANGUAGE DEVELOPMENT IN ENGLISH...46

SKILL 4.1   Know applicable Texas Essential Knowledge and Skills (TEKS), especially the English Language Arts and Reading curriculum as it relates to ESL, and know how to design and implement appropriate instruction to address TEKS related to the listening and speaking strands 46

SKILL 4.2   Understand the role of the linguistic environment and
                   conversational support in second-language development, and use
                   this knowledge to provide a rich, comprehensible language
                   environment with supported opportunities for communication in
                   English 47

SKILL 4.3   Apply knowledge of practices, resources, and materials that are
                   effective in promoting students' communicative competence in
                   English 49

SKILL 4.4   Understand the interrelatedness of listening, speaking, reading, and
                   writing, and use this knowledge to select and use effective
                   strategies for developing students' oral language proficiency in
                   English 52

SKILL 4.5   Apply knowledge of effective strategies for helping ESL students
                   transfer language skills from L1 to L2..54

SKILL 4.6   Apply knowledge of individual differences (e.g., developmental
                   characteristics, cultural and language background, academic
                   strengths, learning styles) to select instructional strategies and
                   resources that facilitate communicative language development........56

SKILL 4.7   Know how to provide appropriate feedback in response to
                   students' developing English language skills 56

COMPETENCY 5   THE ESL TEACHER UNDERSTANDS HOW TO PROMOTE
                   STUDENTS' LITERACY DEVELOPMENT IN ENGLISH........................57

SKILL 5.1   Know applicable Texas Essential Knowledge and Skills (TEKS),
                   especially the English Language Arts and Reading curriculum as it
                   relates to ESL, and know how to design and implement appropriate
                   instruction to address TEKS related to the reading and writing
                   strands 57

SKILL 5.2   Understand the interrelatedness of listening, speaking, reading, and
                   writing, and use this knowledge to select and use effective
                   strategies for developing students' literacy in English 60

SKILL 5.3   Understand that English is an alphabetic language and apply
                   effective strategies for developing ESL students' phonological
                   knowledge and skills (e.g., phonemic awareness skills, knowledge
                   of English letter-sound associations, knowledge of common
                   English phonograms) and sight-word vocabularies (e.g.,
                   phonetically irregular words, high-frequency words)....................61

SKILL 5.4   Know factors that affect ESL students' reading comprehension (e.g., vocabulary, text structures, cultural references) and apply effective strategies for facilitating ESL students' reading comprehension in English..62

SKILL 5.5   Apply knowledge of effective strategies for helping students transfer literacy knowledge and skills from L1 to L2.......................64

SKILL 5.6   Apply knowledge of individual differences (e.g., developmental characteristics, cultural and language background, academic strengths, learning styles) to select instructional strategies and resources that facilitate ESL students' literacy development...........65

SKILL 5.7   Know personal factors that affect ESL students' English literacy development (e.g., interrupted schooling, literacy status in primary language, prior literacy experiences) and apply effective strategies for addressing those factors 66

COMPETENCY 6   THE ESL TEACHER UNDERSTANDS HOW TO PROMOTE STUDENTS' CONTENT-AREA LEARNING, ACADEMIC-LANGUAGE DEVELOPMENT, AND ACHIEVEMENT ACROSS THE CURRICULUM...68

SKILL 6.1   Apply knowledge of effective practices, resources, and materials for providing content-based ESL instruction; engaging students in critical thinking; and developing students' cognitive-academic language proficiency...68

SKILL 6.2   Know instructional delivery practices that are effective in facilitating ESL students' comprehension in content-area classes (e.g., preteaching key vocabulary; helping students apply familiar concepts from their cultural backgrounds and prior experiences to new learning; using hands-on and other experiential learning strategies; using realia, media, and other visual supports to introduce and/or reinforce concepts) 71

SKILL 6.3   Apply knowledge of individual differences (e.g., developmental characteristics, cultural and language background, academic strengths, learning styles) to select instructional strategies and resources that facilitate ESL students' cognitive-academic language development and content-area learning.......................72

SKILL 6.4   Know personal factors that affect ESL students' content-area learning (e.g., prior learning experiences, familiarity with specialized language and vocabulary, familiarity with the structure and uses of textbooks and other print resources) and apply effective strategies for addressing those factors 74

COMPETENCY 7   THE ESL TEACHER UNDERSTANDS FORMAL AND INFORMAL ASSESSMENT PROCEDURES AND INSTRUMENTS USED IN ESL PROGRAMS AND USES ASSESSMENT RESULTS TO PLAN AND ADAPT INSTRUCTION...76

SKILL 7.1   Know basic concepts, issues, and practices related to test design, development, and interpretation, and use this knowledge to select, adapt, and develop assessments for different purposes in the ESL program (e.g., diagnosis, program evaluation, proficiency).............76

SKILL 7.2   Apply knowledge of formal and informal assessments used in the ESL classroom and know their characteristics, uses, and limitations78

SKILL 7.3   Know standardized tests commonly used in ESL programs in Texas and know how to interpret their results.................................81

SKILL 7.4   Know state-mandated Limited English Proficient (LEP) policies, including the role of the Language Proficiency Assessment Committee (LPAC), and procedures for implementing LPAC recommendations for LEP identification, placement, and exit 83

SKILL 7.5   Understand relationships among state-mandated standards, instruction, and assessment in the ESL classroom 84

SKILL 7.6   Know how to use ongoing assessment to plan and adjust instruction that addresses individual student needs and enables ESL students to achieve learning goals 85

DOMAIN III   **FOUNDATIONS OF ESL EDUCATION, CULTURAL AWARENESS, AND FAMILY AND COMMUNITY INVOLVEMENT**...87

COMPETENCY 8   THE ESL TEACHER UNDERSTANDS THE FOUNDATIONS OF ESL EDUCATION AND TYPES OF ESL PROGRAMS 87

SKILL 8.1   Know the historical, theoretical, and policy foundations of ESL education and use this knowledge to plan, implement, and advocate for effective ESL programs 87

SKILL 8.2   Know types of ESL programs (e.g., self-contained, pull-out, newcomer centers, dual-language, and immersion), their characteristics, their goals, and research findings on their effectiveness...89

SKILL 8.3   Apply knowledge of the various types of ESL programs to make appropriate instructional and management decisions 92

SKILL 8.4   Apply knowledge of research findings related to ESL education, including research on instructional and management practices in ESL programs, to assist in planning and implementing effective ESL programs 93

COMPETENCY 9   THE ESL TEACHER UNDERSTANDS FACTORS THAT AFFECT ESL STUDENTS' LEARNING AND IMPLEMENTS STRATEGIES FOR CREATING AN EFFECTIVE MULTICULTURAL AND MULTILINGUAL LEARNING ENVIRONMENT 95

SKILL 9.1   Understand cultural and linguistic diversity in the ESL classroom and other factors that may affect students' learning of academic content, language, and culture (e.g., age, developmental characteristics, academic strengths and needs, preferred learning styles, personality, sociocultural factors, home environment, attitude, exceptionalities) 95

SKILL 9.2   Know how to create an effective multicultural and multilingual learning environment that addresses the affective, linguistic, and cognitive needs of ESL students and facilitates students' learning and language acquisition 98

SKILL 9.3   Know factors that contribute to cultural bias (e.g., stereotyping, prejudice, ethnocentrism) and know how to create a culturally responsive learning environment 98

SKILL 9.4   Demonstrate sensitivity to students' diverse cultural and socioeconomic backgrounds and show respect for language differences 100

SKILL 9.5   Apply strategies for creating among students an awareness of and respect for linguistic and cultural diversity 101

COMPETENCY 10   THE ESL TEACHER KNOWS HOW TO SERVE AS AN ADVOCATE FOR ESL STUDENTS AND FACILITATE FAMILY AND COMMUNITY INVOLVEMENT IN THEIR EDUCATION 102

SKILL 10.1   Apply knowledge of effective strategies advocating educational and social equity for ESL students (e.g., participating in LPAC and ARD meetings, serving on SBDM committees, serving as a resource for teachers) 102

SKILL 10.2   Understand the importance of family involvement in the education of ESL students and know how to facilitate parent/guardian participation in their children's education and school activities........102

SKILL 10.3   Apply skills for communicating and collaborating effectively with the parents/guardians of ESL students in a variety of educational contexts 103

SKILL 10.4   Know how community members and resources can positively affect student learning in the ESL program and be able to access community resources to enhance the education of ESL students.. 104

GLOSSARY OF ABBREVIATIONS AND ACRONYMS 105

BIBLIOGRAPHY 108

SAMPLE TEST 1 114

Answer Key and Rigor Table 134

Answers with Rationales 135

DOMAIN I   LANGUAGE COMPETENCY AND LANGUAGE ACQUISITION

COMPETENCY 1

THE ESL TEACHER UNDERSTANDS FUNDAMENTAL CONCEPTS AND KNOWS THE STRUCTURE AND CONVENTIONS OF THE ENGLISH LANGUAGE

SKILL 1.1   **Understand the nature of language and basic concepts of language systems (e.g., phonology, morphology, syntax, lexicon, semantics, discourse, pragmatics) and use this understanding to facilitate student learning in the ESL classroom**

A teacher of **English as a Second Language (ESL)** or **English for Speakers of Other Languages (ESOL)** must understand basic concepts of language systems. The following is a review of some of the most important ones.

Phonology

The definition of **phonology** can be summarized as "the way in which speech sounds form patterns" (Díaz-Rico & Weed, 2013). Phonology is a subset of the linguistics field, which studies the organization and systems of sound within a particular language. Phonology is based on the theory that every native speaker unconsciously retains the sound structure of his or her language and is more concerned with the sounds than with the physical process of creating those sounds.

When babies babble or make what we call baby sounds, they are actually experimenting with all the sounds represented in all languages. As they learn a specific language, they become more proficient in the sounds of that language and forget how to make sounds that they don't need or use.

Phonology analyzes the sound structure of the given language by

- Determining which phonetic sounds have the most significance
- Explaining how these sounds influence a native speaker of the language

For example, the Russian alphabet has a consonant that, when pronounced, sounds like the French word *rouge*. English speakers typically have difficulty pronouncing this sound pattern, because inherently they know that this is not a typical English-language sound— although it is encountered occasionally (Díaz-Rico & Weed, 2013).

Mastering a sound that does not occur in the learner's first language requires ongoing repetition, both of hearing the sound and attempting to say it. The older the learner, the more difficult this process becomes, especially if the learner has spoken only one language before reaching puberty. Correct pronunciation may require years of practice because initially the learner may not hear the sound correctly.

Expecting an **English language learner (ELL)** to master an English pronunciation quickly leads to frustration for the teacher and the learner. With enough focused repetition, however, the learner may eventually hear the difference and be able to imitate it. Inadequate listening and speaking practice will result in a persistent heavy accent.

Phonemes, pitch, and stress are all components of phonology. Because each affects the meaning being communicated, they are variables that ELLs must recognize and learn.

Phonemes

A **phoneme** is the smallest unit of sound that affects meaning—that is, distinguishes one word from another. In English, there are approximately 44 speech sounds yet only 26 letters, so the sounds, when combined, become words. For this reason, English is not considered a phonetic language—a language of one-to-one correspondence between letters and sounds. For example, consider the two words *pin* and *bin*. The only difference is the first consonant of the words, the "p" in *pin* and "b" in *bin*. The sounds "p" and "b" are phonemes in spoken English, because the difference in sound creates a difference in meaning.

Focusing on phonemes to provide pronunciation practice allows students to have fun while they learn to recognize and say sounds. Pairs or groups of words that have a set pattern make learning easier. For example, students can practice saying words that rhyme but begin with a different phoneme, such as *tan, man, fan, ran*. Other groups of words might start with the same phoneme followed by various vowel sounds, such as *ten, ton, tan, tin*. This kind of alliteration can be used to compose tongue twisters that students find challenging and fun.

Vowels and consonants should be introduced in a deliberate order to allow combinations that form real words, though made-up words that have no real meaning in English may also be used when introducing new sounds.

Pitch

Pitch in communication determines the context or meaning of words or series of words. A string of words can communicate more than one meaning when posed as a question or statement. For example, the phrase "I can't go" acts as a statement if the pitch or intonation falls. However, the same phrase becomes the question "I can't go?" if the pitch or intonation rises for the word *go*.

Stress

Stress can occur at the word or sentence level. At the word level, different stresses on the syllable can actually modify the word's meaning. Consider the word *conflict.* To pronounce it as a noun, one would stress the first syllable, as in **CON-***flict.* However, when used as a verb, the second syllable would be stressed, as in *con-**FLICT.*** Different dialects sometimes pronounce the same word differently, even though both pronunciations have the same meaning. For example, in some parts of the United States the word *insurance* is pronounced by stressing the second syllable, whereas in other parts of the country the first syllable is stressed.

At the sentence level, stress can also be used to vary the meaning. For example, consider the following questions and how the meaning changes, according to the stressed words:

> *He* did that? (Emphasis is on the person.)
> He *did* that? (Emphasis is on the action.)
> He did *that?* (Emphasis is on object of the action.)

This type of meaning differentiation is difficult for most ELLs to grasp, and requires innovative teaching methods, such as acting out the three different meanings. However, since pitch and stress can change the meaning of a sentence completely, students must learn to recognize these differences. Not recognizing sarcasm or anger can cause students considerable problems in their academic endeavors and daily interactions.

Phonographemics

The term **phonographemics** refers to the study of letters and letter combinations. Unlike Spanish and French and many other languages, in English one symbol can represent many phonemes, and there are multiple pronunciations of vowels and consonants. Phonetic rules are critical to learning to read and write; however, because of the numerous exceptions, the rules themselves do little to assist listening and speaking skills, which makes English a difficult language to learn.

When teaching ELLs, it is important to recognize that the wide variation of phonemes represented by a single symbol must be taught and *drilled.* If it is difficult for native speakers to learn the English spelling system, it is a great leap for the nonnative speaker. **Graphemes,** the written letter or group of letters that represents a single sound, should be introduced long after spoken English. Students must first be able to speak and hear the language before they can be taught to spell it. The phonology of spoken English is an important component of an ESOL program.

Phonographemic differences between English words are a common source of confusion and thus need to be taught explicitly with numerous learning activities in order to enable learners to sufficiently understand the various distinctions. Some areas of focus for the ESOL classroom include **homonyms.** Homonyms is a general term for a group of words that are spelled and sound alike or words that are spelled the same, but have two or more meanings. There are three types of homonyms:

- **Homographs:** Two or more words that have the same spelling or pronunciation, but different meanings [e.g., stalk (part of a plant) / stalk (follow)]

- **Homophones:** Two or more words that have the same pronunciation, but have different meanings and spellings (e.g., wood/would, cite/sight)

- **Heteronyms:** Two or more words that have the same spelling, but have a different pronunciation and meaning (e.g., Polish/polish)

Some useful activities for instruction would be to identify misspelled words, to recognize multiple meanings of words in sentences, to spell words correctly within a given context, and to match words with their meanings.

Morphology

Morphology refers to the process of how the words of a language are formed to create meaningful messages. ESOL teachers need to be aware of the principles of morphology in English in order to provide meaningful activities that will help in the process of language learning.

Morphemic analysis requires breaking down a word into its component parts to determine its meaning. It shows the relationship between the root or base word and the prefix and/or suffix to determine the word's meaning.

A **morpheme** is the smallest unit of a language system that has meaning. These units are more commonly known as the root word, the prefix, and the suffix; and they cannot be broken down into any smaller units.

- The **root word** or **base word** is the key to understanding a word, because this is where the actual meaning is determined.

- A **prefix** is a syllable or syllables that appear in front of the root or base word and can alter the meaning of the root or base word.

- A **suffix** is a letter or letters that are added to the end of the word and can alter the original tense or meaning of the root or base word.

The following is an example of how morphemic analysis can be applied to a word:

- Choose a root or base word, such as *kind.*
- Create as many new words as possible, by changing the prefix and suffix.
- New words would include **unkind, kindness,** and *kindly.*

Learning common roots, prefixes, and suffixes greatly helps ELLs to decode unfamiliar words. This approach can make a big difference in how well a student understands written language. Students who can decode unfamiliar words become less frustrated when reading in English and, as a result, are likely to enjoy reading more. They have greater comprehension and their language skills improve more quickly. Having the tools to decode unfamiliar words enables ELLs to perform better on standardized tests because they are more likely to understand the question and the answer choices.

Guessing at the meaning of words should be encouraged. Too often, students become dependent on translation dictionaries, which can cause students to fail to develop morphemic analysis skills. Practice should include identifying roots, prefixes, and suffixes as well as using morphemic knowledge to form new words.

ESOL learners need to understand the structure of words in English, and how words may be created and altered. Some underlying principles of the morphology of English are the following:

1. Morphemes may be free and able to stand by themselves (e.g., chair, bag), or they may be bound or derivational, needing to be used with other morphemes to create meaning (e.g., dis-able, un-able).

2. Knowledge of the meanings of derivational morphemes such as prefixes and suffixes enables students to decode word meanings and create words in the language through word analysis (e.g., un-happy means _not happy_).

3. Some morphemes in English provide grammatical rather than semantic information to words and sentences (e.g., of, the, and).

4. Words can be combined in English to create new compound words (e.g., _key + chain = keychain_).

ESOL teachers also need to be aware that principles of morphology from the native language may be transferred to either promote or interfere with the second-language learning process.

When students overgeneralize a learned rule or simply make a mistake, corrections should be made in a way that does not embarrass the student. Teachers must also consider a student's stage of progress and the context of the error. Correcting every single error is unnecessary when students are experimenting with language and bravely trying to use a language they are struggling to learn. A useful technique is to repeat segments of spoken language, as if to confirm understanding, and correct any errors. This approach saves face for the student and allows the teacher to demonstrate the correct word use or pronunciation. If the student fails to notice the correction and makes the same error again, the teacher can repeat the same type of correction. Teachers can also demonstrate variations of words in this manner, such as using a different verb tense to paraphrase what was said.

Correcting every error in a writing sample can discourage participation and cause students to shut down to learning. Keeping track of errors that students repeat allows the teacher to reteach specific skills or address specific needs, either with a group of students who all need to master that skill or individually for a student who has not yet mastered a skill with others in the class.

Syntax

Syntax involves the order in which words are arranged to create meaning. Different languages use different patterns for sentence structure. Syntax also refers to the rules for creating correct sentence patterns. English, like many other languages, is a **subject-verb-object (SVO)** language, which means that in most sentences the subject precedes the verb, and the object follows the verb. ELLs whose native language follows an SVO sentence structure will find it easier to master English syntax.

Language acquisition is a gradual, hierarchical, and cumulative process. This means that learners must go through and master each stage in sequence, much as Piaget theorized for learning in general. In terms of syntax, this means learners must acquire specific grammatical structures, first recognizing the difference between subject and predicate; putting subject before predicate; and then learning more complex variations, such as questions, negatives, and relative clauses.

Although learners must pass through each stage and accumulate the language skills learned progressively, learners use different approaches to mastering these skills. Some learners use more cognitive-processing procedures, which means that more of their learning takes place through thought processes. Other learners tend to use psycholinguistic procedures, processing and learning through more speaking.

Regardless of how learners process information, they must all proceed through the same stages, from the least to the most complicated. Experts disagree on the exact definition of the phases, but a set of six general stages would include the following:

Stage of Development	Examples
1. Single words	I; throw; ball
2. SVO structure	I throw the ball.
3. *Wh*-fronting *Do* fronting Adverb fronting Negative + verb	Where you are? Do you like me? Today I go to school. She is not nice.
4. Y/N inversion Copula (linking verb) inversion Particle shift	Do you know him? Yes, I know him. Is he at school? Take your hat off.

5. *Do* 2nd   Why did she leave?
Auxiliary 2nd   Where has he gone?
Negative *do* 2nd   She does not live here.

6. Cancel inversion   I asked what she was doing.

Each progressive step requires the learner to use knowledge from the previous step as well as new knowledge of the language. As ELLs progress to more advanced stages of syntax, they may react differently, depending on their ability to acquire the new knowledge that is required for mastery. They progress more rapidly through the stages than they did when learning their native language.

Semantics

Semantics encompasses the meaning of individual words, as well as combinations of words. Native speakers use their language to function in their daily lives at all levels. Through experience, they know the effects of intonation, connotation, and synonyms. In an ESOL class, we are trying to teach nonnative speakers as quickly as possible what the native speaker already knows. The objectives of beginning ESOL lesson plans should deliberately build a foundation that will enable students to meet more advanced objectives.

Teaching within a specific context helps students to understand the meaning of words and sentences. When students can remember the context in which they learned words and recall how the words were used, they retain that knowledge and can compare it with different applications of the same words as they are introduced.

Using words in a variety of contexts helps students reach deeper understandings of the words. They can then guess at new meanings that are introduced in different contexts. For example, the word *conduct* can be taught in the context of conducting a meeting or an investigation. Later the word *conductor* can be used in various contexts that demonstrate some similarity but have distinctly different uses of the word, such as a conductor of electricity, the conductor of a train, the conductor of an orchestra, and so forth.

Second-language learners must learn to translate words and sentences that they already understand in their primary language into the language they wish to acquire. This can be a daunting task because of the many ways meaning is created in English. Voice inflection, variations of meaning, variations of usage, and emphasis are some of the factors that affect meaning. The **lexicon** of language includes the stored meaning and contextual meaning from word association, as well as knowledge of pronunciation, grammar, and morphemes.

Discourse

The term **discourse** refers to linguistic units composed of several sentences and is derived from the concept of **discursive formation,** communication that involves specialized knowledge of various kinds. Discourse plays a role in all spoken and written language. It shapes the way language is transmitted and how we organize our thoughts. Conversations, arguments, and speeches are types of **spoken discourse.**

The structure of discourse varies among languages and traditions. For example, Japanese writing does not present the main idea at the beginning of an essay; rather, writing builds up to the main idea, which is presented or implied at the end of the essay. This structure is completely different from English writing, which typically presents the main idea or thesis at the beginning of an essay and repeats it at the end.

In addition to language and structure, topic—or focus—affects discourse. The discourse in various disciplines (such as feminist studies, cultural studies, and literary theory) approaches topics differently.

Discourse between speakers of English requires knowledge of certain protocols in addition to other aspects of spoken language. Speakers should have the necessary skills to maintain the momentum of a conversation, as well as to correct misunderstandings. Typical spoken discourse follows predictable patterns. For example, one person might say, "I saw a good movie last night." The other person would ask, "What was it about?" The first person then answers in a paragraph with a topic sentence, "It was about a bunch of guys who devised a plan to rob a casino," and then proceeds to fill in the details.

Vocal Discourse

Vocal discourse varies significantly depending on context. People speak in different styles depending on who they are talking to and what the occasion demands. A candidate who is running for president and speaking to a group will use more formal speech than in a casual conversation. The message conveyed may also vary, depending on whether the group is one of supporters or people who hold different political views. In either case, the candidate must make choices about how to organize what he or she says to ensure comprehension and to hold the audience's interest.

ELLs might initially practice set conversations to learn the patterns of English discourse. Practicing in pairs, using a question-and-answer format, gives both participants an opportunity to learn the structures of discourse as well as information about the other person or the other person's culture. Such practice also gives students practice with other language skills and can increase vocabulary. The teacher may provide a set of questions and learners can alternate asking and answering. Short skits that repeat a limited number of words also provide helpful practice. Allowing students time to converse informally, perhaps using suggested topics, continues to reinforce speech patterns.

Polite Discourse

Polite discourse includes what is called "empty language" or perfunctory speech that has little meaning but is important in social exchanges. Frequently English speakers start a conversation by asking, "How are you?" even though they have no real interest in the other person's health. An appropriate response would be, "Fine," even if the person may not feel well. The exchange is simply a polite means of greeting a person or starting a conversation.

Likewise, at the end of a discourse empty language is frequently employed: "It was good to see you." "Good to see you, too." This type of discourse is considered to be part of the **Basic Interpersonal Communication Skills (BICS)** that learners must acquire to function in social situations (Cummins, 1998). It is generally less demanding than **Cognitive Academic Language Proficiency (CALP)**, and allows learners to participate in informal conversations.

Written Discourse

Written discourse ranges from the most basic grouping of sentences to the most complicated essays and stories. Regardless of the level, English writing demands certain structural patterns. A typical paragraph begins with a topic sentence, which states directly or indirectly the focus of the paragraph, adds supporting ideas and details, and ends with a concluding sentence that relates to the focus and either states the final thought on that topic or provides a transition to the next paragraph when there are more than one. As with spoken discourse, organization, tone, and word choice are critical to transferring thoughts successfully and maintaining interest.

As skills increase, paragraphs are combined into stories or essays. Each type of writing has specific components and structures. Story writing requires setting, plot, and character. Initially, following a chronological order is probably easiest for ELLs. However, as learners become more skillful other types of order should be practiced—for example, adding descriptions in spatial order.

Teachers frequently rely on the proverbial three- to five-paragraph structure to teach essay writing because it provides a framework for organizing and expanding ideas within a single focus. It mirrors the paragraph structure organizationally in that the first, or introductory, paragraph provides the main idea or focus of the essay; each body paragraph develops a supporting idea and adds details; and the concluding paragraph provides a summary or other type of conclusion that relates to the main idea or focus stated in the first paragraph.

Obviously, no one considers such a mechanical writing format to be the ultimate goal of essay writing. However, especially for ELLs, having a rigid structure teaches the basic organizational concept of English-language essays. By offering strictly defined limits, the teacher reduces the number of variables to learn about essay writing. Starting with a blank page can be overwhelming to ELLs. Working within an organized structure enables learners to focus on developing each paragraph—a challenging enough task, when one considers the language skills required! As learners gain the facility to control their writing and sustain a focus, variations can be introduced and topics expanded.

Language proficiency requires both BICS and CALP. While they have clear distinctions, they also have underlying similarities that contribute to overall language learning. In addition, students should also recognize **Common Underlying Proficiency (CUP).** These are skills, ideas, and concepts that learners can transfer from their first language to their English learning. Similarities and differences between languages can both help learners comprehend and learn aspects of English.

Pragmatics

Pragmatics is the study of how the context impacts the interpretation of language. Situations dictate language choice, body language, the degree of intimacy, and how meaning is interpreted. For example, when customers walk into a bar and sit down on stools, they expect a bartender will ask them several questions: "What would you like to drink?" and "Would you like to start a tab?" This sequence of events and cues is a typical pattern of interaction in a bar. Pragmatic knowledge provides the customer with a set of expectations for the flow of events. Typically, people in a bar expect a certain level of social exchange that allows congeniality without intrusiveness. They expect to receive a certain level of service, and to use a particular level of manners. These types of exchanges are fairly universal in bars but would be completely inappropriate in a more formal setting (for example, when conversing with the president of a corporation).

Gestures, the appropriate distance between speakers, seating arrangements, nodding and shaking of the head, signs, and touch are all examples of nonverbal pragmatic conventions. These elements differ from culture to culture and may be taught.

In the ESL classroom, pragmatics can be illustrated and practiced by repeating the same situation in different contexts. For example, students can write or act out how they would explain why they failed a test to three different people: their best friend, their teacher, and their parent. With a little imagination, different scenarios can be chosen that pique student interest and make learning fun. For example, explain an embarrassing event in different contexts, such as in front of a boy or girl you want to impress, a close friend, and an authority figure. For students with very low language skills, pantomime can encourage participation, teach the concept, and create an opportunity for using language to describe what has happened.

For students from other cultures, pragmatics involving nonverbal cues and body language can be confusing. It is the teacher's responsibility to be sensitive to these different behaviors and acknowledge them when they become obvious in the classroom, and to guide students to adopt behaviors appropriate to their audience, purpose, and setting.

Students may be unaware that others feel uncomfortable because they are standing too close or not making eye contact. These situations are very common examples of cultural differences in nonverbal communication. The problem could be addressed directly by discussing appropriate behaviors in different cultures, perhaps by focusing on behavior appropriate to the teacher as a model.

Other examples of nonverbal communication are gestures, tone, volume, stress, and intonation. Appropriate use varies in different social settings. All students (and not just ELLs) need to learn the appropriate voice volume for different settings such as the library, hall, gymnasium, supermarket, and movie theater. An appropriate correction for young children would be to ask all the class members to use their "inside" voices and not their "outside" (playground) voices when speaking in the classroom.

SKILL 1.2   **Know the functions and registers of language (e.g., social versus academic languages) in English and use this knowledge to develop and modify instructional materials, deliver instruction, and promote ESL students' English language proficiency**

American English usage is influenced by the social and regional situation of its users. Linguists have found that speakers adapt their pronunciation, vocabulary, grammar, and sentence structure depending on the social situation. For example, the decision to use "ing" or "in" at the end of a present participle depends on the formality of the situation. Speakers talking with their friends will often drop the "g" and use "in" to signal that the situation is more informal and relaxed. These variations are also related to factors such as age, gender, education, socioeconomic status, and personality.

We call this type of shift a change in **language register,** how language is used in a particular setting or for a particular purpose. People change their speech register depending on such sociolinguistic variables as

- Formality of situation
- Attitude toward topic
- Attitude toward listeners
- Relation of speaker to others

Changing speech registers may be completely subconscious for native speakers. For example, if a university professor takes her car in for servicing, the manner and speech she uses to communicate with the mechanic differs significantly from the manner and speech she uses to deliver a lecture. If she were to use a formal tone and academic vocabulary, the mechanic might think the professor was trying to put him down, or he might not understand what the professor was saying. Likewise, when the mechanic explains the mechanical diagnosis, he most likely chooses a simplified vocabulary rather than using completely technical language, or jargon, that the professor wouldn't understand. Using the jargon of a profession or field with which the listener is unfamiliar will likely make the listener feel stupid or inferior, and perhaps make him or her think that the speaker is inconsiderate.

Social Language

Language registers are also used to deliberately establish a social identity. Hispanics deliberately refer to themselves as *La Raza* (the race) to imply dignity and pride for who they are and where they come from. Using a Spanish term when speaking English is called **code switching.** This term has become a part of the American vocabulary. Symbolically it represents both the Hispanics' distinction and their integration into American culture.

ESOL teachers should be aware of these sociolinguistic functions of language and compare different social functions of language for their students. Knowing and being able to use appropriate registers allows learners to function more effectively in social situations. Learners must acquire the social, as well as the linguistic, aspects of American English. Sociolinguistic functions of a language are best acquired by using the language in authentic situations.

Sociolinguistic diversity, language variations based on regional and social differences, affects teachers' language, attitudes, and practices. Teachers must respect the validity of any group's or individual's language patterns while at the same time teaching traditional English. Vernacular versions of English have well-established patterns and rules to support them. Making learners aware of language variations leads to increased interest in language learning and better ability to switch among one or more registers or dialects and standard English.

ELLs tend to adapt linguistic structures to their familiar culture, modifying specific concepts and practices. Teachers must identify these variations, call attention to them, and teach the appropriate English equivalent. The goal is not to eliminate linguistic diversity, but rather to enable learners to control their language use so that they can willfully use standard English *in addition to* their cultural variation.

Various functional adaptations of English have great significance to the cultural groups that use them. Attempting to eliminate variations not only is futile, but raises hostility and reluctance to learn English. Stable, socially shared structures emerge from the summed effects of many individual communication practices. Firmly ingrained language patterns serve a purpose within the community that uses them. Unique variations can arise in a school venue. New, nonstandard English words can represent a particular group's identity or function as a means to solidify social relationships. As long as students recognize that a variation should not be used as if it were standard English, there should be no problem with its use.

Academic Discourse

Academic discourse refers to formal academic learning. This includes all four language skills: listening, reading, speaking, and writing. Academic learning is important in order for students to succeed in school. Cummins differentiated between two types of language proficiency: BICS and CALP (see Skill 1.1). An average student can acquire BICS within two to five years of language learning whereas CALP can take from four to seven years. Many factors are involved in the acquisition of CALP, such as age, language proficiency level, literacy in the first language, and so forth.

Explicit instruction of some key language skills—vocabulary, grammar, and genre—should be provided to students to help them learn academic discourse in order for them to succeed in a school setting.

Academic discourse includes knowledge of content-area vocabulary and the various skills and strategies that are essential to successfully complete academic tasks in a mainstream classroom. Some of these skills and strategies are inferring, classifying, analyzing, synthesizing, and evaluating. As students reach higher grades, they are required to think critically and apply this knowledge to solve problems.

With respect to reading and writing, complex grammatical structures are frequently found in academic discourse, which makes it challenging for ELLs. In addition, science and other subject-area textbooks normally employ the use of the passive voice. Similarly, the use of reference, pronouns, modals, and so on is a common feature of academic discourse that might cause problems for ELLs. All the language features of academic discourse help to convey the intended meaning of the author; therefore, it is necessary to explicitly teach them in order for students to become skilled readers and writers.

Genre is an important aspect of academic discourse. Each genre employs a style of writing that is unique unto itself. The organization of a text structure differs according to the purpose of the text—for example, mystery versus romance. Likewise, in academic reading, students come across multiple texts that vary in organization and style according to the purpose of the author and according to the intended audience. Students need to understand the different features of multiple texts to become efficient readers. With respect to writing, students need to determine the purpose of their writing (e.g., argumentative writing versus story writing).

SKILL 1.3   **Understand the interrelatedness of listening, speaking, reading, and writing and use the understanding to develop ESL students' English language proficiency**

Phonological awareness is a significant part of literacy development in children. Likewise, research has shown that phonological awareness also plays an important role as children with limited English language proficiency learn to read both in their **first or native language (L1)** and in their **second language (L2).** Students need to understand the words in order to read texts. To read words, they need to be aware of the letters and the sounds represented by letters. This basic learning results in the blending of sounds that helps them to pronounce words. Reading educators have found that phonological awareness is critical to the development of comprehension skills.

Furthermore, when **fluency in word recognition** is achieved, the child focuses more on understanding what is read. Therefore, researchers emphasize the importance of word recognition instruction to enhance fluency. It is recommended that educators who want to improve students' comprehension skills first teach them how to decode well. Explicit instruction in sounding out words is a start in developing good comprehension skills.

Word recognition skills must be developed to the point of fluency if comprehension is to be increased.

Research has shown that phonological awareness in the native language (i.e., L1) of the English language learners predicts successful literacy acquisition of both L1 and L2. Therefore, the closer the phonologies of L1 and L2, the more likely it is that the transfer of skills will help ELLs in their literacy development of L2. Studies suggest beginning instruction for bilingual children with the sounds and patterns that the two languages share. Teachers can then move on to the sounds and patterns that are different between the two languages. In this way, teachers can build upon the transfer of the common sounds of both languages in order to help their students achieve literacy skills. Instruction could follow with discussion of the sounds that are different between the two languages, to avoid negative transfer.

In short, phonological awareness of both the native language and the target language can help increase the literacy skills of an ELL. This awareness not only fosters word recognition skills and fluency but also helps students focus their cognitive capabilities on increasing their reading comprehension.

Integrating the Four Language Skills

Integration of all four language skills is beneficial for all ELLs, regardless of their proficiency level (Genesee et al., 2006). This integration provides an effective context for writing so that the use of one skill leads naturally to the use of another, as in real life. In this way, learners will see how writing relates to certain communicative needs just as the other skills do. For example, students need to participate in classroom conversations by articulating their opinions, sharing their observations, making comparisons, and so on, through speaking and writing. They need to listen to the topic, take notes, discuss with their classmates, and read about the topic, which requires the integration of all four skills.

Activities should be organized to encourage ELLs to use all four language skills needed to engage in real-life communicative situations. In order to do this, students should speak not only with the teacher but also with other students. The student will also listen and try to comprehend what other speakers are saying. The listener can then react by writing down for a reader his version of the information he has just heard. This sequence of activities helps ELLs brainstorm ideas in the target language before they put them on paper, thereby providing some opportunity for the student to translate his or her idea from his or her native language into English. In this scenario, prewriting techniques give the students opportunity to use all of the four skills to help them explore and initiate their ideas on a given topic, or to develop a topic for a writing activity based on communication activities in the classroom.

Brainstorming

Brainstorming allows students working together in the classroom in small groups to say as much as they can about a topic, which helps them generate ideas to use in their own brainstorming on paper. Thus, brainstorming uses both speaking and listening skills to produce effective writing.

Guided Discussion

Another way to get students to talk about a topic or to focus on specific aspects of a topic is to provide guidelines for group or whole class discussion. This technique offers the advantage of helping the students beforehand with the vocabulary and sentence forms that they might need in their discussion. This method again makes use of all four skills to guide students in their writing process.

Some of the other activities that encourage students to use the four linguistic skills are the following:

- Interviews
- Skits
- Dictation
- Note taking
- Storytelling

ESL teaching recognizes the importance of giving ELLs integrative tasks that help them achieve their language goals by including any or all of the following language skills: listening, speaking, reading, writing, and viewing. Tasks are loosely defined as any activities that emphasize meaning over form. Which tasks are chosen depends on the teacher, who makes decisions about appropriate tasks for his or her classroom.

Candlin (1987, in Batstone, 1994: 17) suggests that beneficial tasks are those that

- Encourage learners to attend to meaning
- Give learners flexibility in problem solving
- Involve learners whose personality and attitude is primary
- Are challenging but not too demanding
- Raise ELLs' awareness of the process of language use, encouraging them to reflect on their own language use

Tasks can be divided into two different types. **Learning tasks** are those that focus on formal features of language and have specific learning outcomes. **Communicative tasks** are typically focused on meaning and are frequently open-ended. Often they are used in group work and may have a written component which summarizes the work.

Tasks also may be classified into three main groups:

1. **Information-gap tasks** involve the transfer of given information from one person to another, from one form to another, or from one place to another. The activity often involves selection of relevant information, as well, and learners may have to meet criteria of completeness and correctness in making the transfer.

2. **Reasoning-gap tasks** involve deriving some new information from given information through processes of inference, deduction, practical reasoning, or a perception of relationships or patterns.

3. **Opinion-gap tasks** involve identifying and articulating a personal preference, feeling, or attitude in response to a given situation. (Adapted from Prabhu, 1987: 46-47)

Authenticity is an important component of tasks in the classroom. Many instructors and researchers believe that learning tasks should be authentic or use "real" spoken English. According to Nunan (1989) the distinction between real-world tasks and pedagogic tasks may be blurred in reality. He believes that pedagogic activities, while they may seem artificial, may in fact practice enabling skills such as fluency, discourse, and interactional skills, mastery of phonological elements, and mastery of grammar. He suggests that there may be no hard and fast distinction between real-world and pedagogic tasks.

SKILL 1.4   **Know the structure of the English language (e.g., word formation, grammar, sentence structure) and the patterns and conventions of written and spoken English and use this knowledge to model and provide instruction in English**

Subject and Predicate

A sentence is a group of words that has a subject and predicate and expresses a complete idea. A subject tells us what or whom the sentence is about and the predicate makes a statement about what the subject is or does. Subjects and predicates can be modified and combined in different ways to make simple, compound, or complex sentences. (In the following examples, subjects are underlined and predicates are italicized.)

Example: The snow *falls quietly*.

Subject: The subject, or the topic of a sentence, consists of a noun or a pronoun and all the words that modify it. "The snow" is the subject in the above example. The simple subject is the main part of the subject. "Snow" is the simple subject.

Predicate: The predicate makes a statement or a comment about the subject and it consists of a verb and all the words that modify it: "falls quietly" is the predicate in the example above. The simple predicate is the main part of the predicate and is always the verb; "falls" is the simple predicate.

In a **compound subject,** the subject consists of two or more nouns or pronouns.

Example: Books and magazines *filled the room*.

In a **compound predicate,** the predicate contains more than one verb pertaining to the subject.

Example: <u>The boys</u> *walked and talked.*

Types of Sentences

Sentences in English are of three types:

1. **Simple Sentence:** A simple sentence, or independent clause, is a complete thought consisting of a single subject and a single predicate:

   Example: <u>The bus</u> *was late.*

2. **Compound Sentence:** A compound sentence consists of two independent clauses joined together by a conjunction (and, or, nor, but, for, yet, so):

   Example: <u>Tom</u> *walked to the bus station,* **and** <u>he</u> *took the bus.*

3. **Complex Sentence:** A complex sentence is a sentence consisting of a dependent clause (a group words with a subject and predicate that are not a complete thought) and an independent clause, joined together using a subordinator (although, after, when, because, since, while):

   Example: <u>After I</u> *write the report,* <u>I</u> *will submit it to my teacher.*

Sentences serve different purposes. They can make a statement (**declarative**); ask a question (**interrogative**); give a command (**imperative**); or express a sense of urgency (**exclamatory**). Understanding the different purposes for sentences can help ELLs understand the relationship between what they write and the ideas they want to express.

Parts of Speech

ELLs often overgeneralize that sentence fragments are short and complete sentences are long. When they truly understand what constitutes a sentence, they will realize that length has nothing to do with whether a sentence is complete or not. For example:

"He ran." is a complete sentence.
"After the very funny story began" is a fragment.

To make these distinctions, learners must know the parts of speech and understand the difference between independent clauses, dependent clauses, and phrases. A phrase is a group of words that does not have a subject and a predicate and cannot stand alone. The most common types of phrases are prepositional (in the room); participial (walking down the street); and infinitive (to run).

Constructing sentences involves combining words in grammatically correct ways to communicate thoughts. Avoiding fragments and run-ons requires continual sentence analysis. The test of a complete sentence is: Does it contain both a subject and a predicate and express a complete idea? Practice identifying independent clauses, dependent clauses, and phrases will help ELLs to write complete sentences.

Parts of speech include eight classifications for words. Each part of speech has a specific role in sentences. This concept can be difficult for ELLs because the same word can have a different role in different sentences, and a different meaning entirely. Identifying the subject and predicate of the sentence helps to distinguish what role a particular word plays in a sentence. Since English is an SVO language, the placement of a word in a sentence relative to the subject or verb indicates what part of speech it is.

> That TV *show* was boring.
> I will *show* you my new dress.
> The band plays *show* tunes at half-time.

In these examples, the word *show* is first a noun, then a verb, and finally, an adjective.

The parts of speech include the following:

1. **Noun:** a person, place, thing, or idea. Common nouns are nonspecific, while proper nouns name a particular person, place, thing, or idea, and are capitalized.

2. **Verb:** an action or state of being.

3. **Pronoun:** a word that takes the place of a noun. There are three types of pronouns.

   - Personal pronouns are classified as follows:

     First, second, or third person (*I, you, he, she, it*)
     Singular or plural (*I/we, you/you, he, she, it/they*)
     Subjective or objective (*I/me, you/you, he/him, she/her, it/it, we/us, they/them*)

   - Possessive pronouns show ownership (*my, mine, your, yours, his, her, hers, its, our, ours, your, yours, their, theirs*).

   - Indefinite pronouns refer to persons, places, things, or ideas in general (*any, each, both, most, something*).

4. **Adjective:** a word that modifies a noun or pronoun. Adjectives answer the questions *What kind? How many?* and *Which?*

5. Adverb: a word that modifies a verb, an adjective, or another adverb. Adverbs answer the questions *How? When? Where? How often?* and *To what extent?*

6. Preposition: a word that occurs in a phrase with a noun or pronoun and shows the relationship between a noun or pronoun and another word in a sentence. It describes, or shows location, direction, or time. Prepositional phrases can have as few as two words, but can include any number of adjectives. Words such as *under, behind, down, up, before,* and *after* are common prepositions. "Until dark," "unless it rains", and "before we get the table set up," are examples of shorter and longer prepositional phrases.

7. Conjunction: a word that joins words, phrases, clauses, and sentences. Conjunctions are organized into the following groups:

> Coordinating conjunctions: *and, but, for, yet, or, nor,* etc.
> Subordinating conjunctions: *after, because, so that, while, as soon as,* etc.
> Correlative conjunctions: *both…and, either…or, neither…nor,* etc.
> Conjunctive adverbs: *therefore, thus, moreover,* etc.

8. Interjection: a word that shows surprise or strong feeling. It can stand alone (Help!) or be used within a sentence (Oh no! I forgot my wallet!).

Idiomatic Expressions

Idioms are a part of American conversational speech and recreational reading used by native English speakers. Idioms are groups of words that have a new meaning different than the words' original definitions. For example, "You're pulling my leg." Literally, the phrase means that someone is pulling another person's leg. However, as an idiom it has been given a new meaning: "You are kidding, or teasing, me."

Idiomatic expressions are difficult for ELLs and need to be taught in a structured form that incorporates discussions and contextual support. For ELLs, the additional support of illustrating an idiom brings in another strategy for internalizing its meaning. However, idioms are rarely, if ever, found in academic writing or content information, such as history or science textbooks.

More information about idiomatic expressions can be found in Skill 2.5.

Standard Usage

Written English has always employed standard usage. Literacy is the main reason for promoting standard usage. Linguists define standard English as *educated English* or as "the set of grammatical and lexical forms which is typically used in speech and writing by educated native speakers" (Trudgill, 1984). Standard English is considered the proper form of English that is normally used in writing, especially in printed materials. Additionally, it is the form associated with the education system in all of the English-speaking countries of the world; therefore, standard English is spoken by educated people and taught to nonnative learners.

In a formal setting, people normally speak standard, or proper, English. It is normally used in conferences, speeches, interviews, classrooms, business functions, and so on. According to Perera (1993), some features are easily recognized as nonstandard:

- He ain't here. (negative forms)
- They was laughing. (verb forms)
- I want them books. (pronouns)
- He likes the play what I had wrote. (determiners)

Perera also puts forward five characteristics that differentiate spoken standard English from written English.

1. Speech contains false starts, hesitations, mazes, and incomplete sentences that do not usually occur in writing. In addition, much of the speech we listen to (apart from participation in conversations) is actually written or prepared text, such as lectures, sermons, or television and radio content.

2. Speech contains **discourse markers,** such as "well," "you know," "sort of," and "I mean." If speech is deprived of these features, it sounds like a lecture or an address instead of a conversation among equals.

3. Speech depends highly on the context in which it occurs. Meaning is derived from the situation. This means that face-to-face spoken language does not need to be as full or as explicit as written language. For example, this utterance might be said to a delivery carrier: *"Leave it there, please,"* as compared to a written note: *Please leave the ironing board on the porch, in the corner, behind the umbrella stand.*

4. Speech contains characteristic constructions that do not normally occur in writing. For example, increased redundancy makes processing easier for both speaker and listener, such as, "All the people in my office, they can't speak English properly, they can't write English properly."

5. Speech is, on the whole, less formal than writing. When we're writing, we know that what we write may be read by anyone. However, when we speak, we know to whom we are speaking and often know them well. Appropriate use of language entails being able to select the right style for a particular context.

Written standard English, on the other hand, is more formal and explicit in nature. It is used in legal documents, newspapers, books, journals, educational materials, textbooks, and so on. It includes conventions such as word choice, word order, punctuation, and spelling. It is a form of English that is typically used in academic, professional, and business contexts. It is expected of students that they follow the conventions of standard English in their written work. It is important for students to learn traditionally proper

English in order to succeed in an academic setting. In addition, students need to comprehend and evaluate the information that is provided to them in their daily lives through newspapers, magazines, and other media. This helps them to be aware of the world around them and to be responsible citizens.

COMPETENCY 2

THE ESL TEACHER UNDERSTANDS THE PROCESSES OF FIRST-LANGUAGE (L1) AND SECOND-LANGUAGE (L2) ACQUISITION AND THE INTERRELATEDNESS OF L1 AND L2 DEVELOPMENT

SKILL 2.1   Know theories, concepts, and research related to L1 and L2 acquisition

Between two and three years of age, most children develop sufficient language to influence the people closest to them. Research shows that, in general, boys acquire language more slowly than girls, which means teachers need to consider very carefully how they involve boys in activities designed to promote early language and literacy. Various theories have tried to explain the language acquisition process.

Classical Theories and Concepts of Language Acquisition

Chomsky: Language Acquisition Device

Noam Chomsky's theory, described as Nativist, asserts that humans are born with a special biological brain mechanism, called a **Language Acquisition Device (LAD).** His theory supposes that the ability to learn language is innate, that nature is more important than nurture, and that experience using language is necessary only in order to activate the LAD. Chomsky based his assumptions on work in linguistics. His work shows that children's language development is much more complex than that taught by followers of Behaviorist theory, which says that children learn language merely by being rewarded for imitating. However, Chomsky's theory underestimates the influence that thought (cognition) and language have on each other's development.

Piaget: Cognitive Constructivism

Jean Piaget's central interest was children's cognitive development. He theorized that language is simply one way that children represent their familiar worlds; language is a reflection of thought, and does not contribute to the development of thinking. He believed cognitive development precedes language development.

Vygotsky: Social Constructivism and Language

Unlike Chomsky and Piaget, Lev Vygotsky had a central focus on the relationship between the development of thought and language. He was interested in the ways different languages impact a person's thinking. He suggests that what Piaget believed was young children's egocentric speech was actually private speech, and that the child's way of using words to think about something progressed from social speech to thinking in words. Vygotsky viewed language first as social communication, which gradually promotes both language itself and cognition.

Recent Theorizing: Intentionality

Some contemporary researchers and theorists criticize earlier theories and suggest that children, their behaviors, and their attempts to understand and communicate are misunderstood when the causes of language development are thought to be "outside" the child or else mechanistically "in the child's brain." They recognize that children are active learners who co-construct their worlds. Their language development is part of their holistic development, emerging from cognitive, emotional, and social interactions. These theorists believe language development depends on the child's social and cultural environment, the people in it, and their interactions. How children represent these factors in their minds is fundamental to language development. They believe a child's agenda and the interactions generated by the child promote language learning. The adult's role, actions, and speech are still considered important, but adults need to be able to "mind read" and adjust their side of the co-construction to relate to an individual child's understanding and interpretation.

Theories about language development help us to understand that enjoying **proto-conversations** with babies (treating them as people who can understand, share, and have intentions in sensitive interchanges), and truly listening to young children, is the best way to promote their language development.

Brain research has shown that the single most important factor affecting language acquisition is the onset of puberty. Before puberty, a person uses one area of the brain for language learning; after puberty, a different area of the brain is used. A person who learns a second language before reaching puberty will always process language learning as if prepubescent. A person who begins to learn a second language after the onset of puberty will likely find language learning more difficult and will depend more on repetition.

Krashen: Theory of Second-Language Acquisition

Stephen Krashen developed a **theory of second-language acquisition,** which helps explain the processes used by adults when learning a second language:

- **Acquisition-Learning Hypothesis:** There is a difference between learning a language and acquiring it. Children acquire a second language using the same process they used to learn their first language. However, adults who know only one language have to learn a language through coursework, studying, and memorizing. One can acquire a second language, but often it requires more deliberate interaction within that language.

- **Monitor Hypothesis:** The learned language "monitors" the acquired language. This is when a person's "grammar check" kicks in and keeps awkward, incorrect language out of a person's L2 communication.

- **Natural Order Hypothesis:** The learning of grammatical structures is predictable and follows a "natural order."

- **Input Hypothesis:** A language learner will learn best when the instruction or conversation is just above the learner's ability. That way, the learner has the foundation to understand most of the language but will have to figure out, often in context, the unknown elements. Some people call this comprehensible input (see Skill 2.2).

- **Affective Filter Hypothesis:** People will learn a second language when they are relaxed, have high levels of motivation, and have a decent level of self-confidence.

Stages of L1 and L2 Learning

Teaching students who are learning English as a second language poses some unique challenges, particularly in a standards-based environment. Teachers should teach with the student's developmental level in mind. Instruction should not be "dumbed-down" for ELLs. Different approaches should be used to ensure that these students receive multiple opportunities to learn and practice English while learning the content.

L1 and L2 learning both follow many, if not all, of the same steps:

- **Silent period:** The stage when a learner knows perhaps 500 receptive words but feels uncomfortable producing speech. The absence of speech does not indicate a lack of learning and teachers should not try to force the learner to speak. Comprehension can be checked by having the learner point or mime. This is also known as the **receptive** or **preproduction** stage.

- **Private speech:** The learner knows about 1,000 receptive words and speaks in one- or two-word phrases. The learner can use simple responses, such as yes/no, and either/or. This stage is also known as **early production.**

- **Lexical chunks:** The learner knows about 3,000 receptive words and can communicate using short phrases and sentences. Long sentences typically have grammatical errors. This stage is also known as **speech emergence.**

- **Formulaic speech:** The learner knows about 6,000 receptive words and begins to make complex statements, state opinions, ask for clarification, share thoughts, and speak at greater length. This stage is also known as **intermediate language proficiency.**

- **Experimental or simplified speech:** The learner develops a level of fluency and can make semantic and grammar generalizations. This stage is also known as **advanced language proficiency.**

Researchers disagree on whether the development of formulaic speech and experimental or simplified speech is the same for L1 and L2 learners. Regardless, understanding that students must go through a predictable, sequential series of stages helps teachers to recognize the students' progress and respond effectively. Providing comprehensible input will help students advance their language learning at any stage.

SKILL 2.2 **Use knowledge of theories, concepts, and research related to L1 and L2 acquisition to select effective, appropriate methods and strategies for promoting students' English language development at various stages**

In language learning, **input** is defined as the language information or data to which the learner is exposed and has access. Learners receive input from their parents, their teachers, their community, TV, textbooks, readers, audio- and video-tapes, other students in the classroom, and so on.

It is generally accepted that **comprehensible input** is key to second-language learning. Even so, input alone is not considered to lead to second-language acquisition. The "kind" of input must also be taken into consideration.

Krashen believes humans acquire language in only one way: by understanding messages—that is, by receiving comprehensible input. Krashen defines comprehensible input as *i* + 1, or input that is just beyond the learner's present ability. In this way, learners can move from what they know to the next level in the natural order of acquisition.

Other theorists report that frequency of certain items in the target language appears to contribute to output (Dulay & Burt, 1974; Schmidt & Frota, 1986). Virginia Collier (1995) states that her research suggests that classes in schools that are highly interactive, emphasizing student problem solving and discovery through thematic experiences across the curriculum, are likely to provide the kind of social setting for natural language acquisition to take place simultaneously with academic and cognitive development. She continues, "Collaborative interaction in which meaning is negotiated with peers is central to the language acquisition process, for both oral and written language development."

SKILL 2.3 **Know cognitive processes (e.g., memorization, categorization, generalization, metacognition) involved in synthesizing and internalizing language rules for second-language acquisition**

Cognitive Strategies

Cognitive strategies are vital to second-language acquisition; their most salient feature is the manipulation of the second language. The most basic strategies are practicing, receiving and sending messages, analyzing and reasoning, and creating structure for input and output. These strategies can be remembered by the acronym **PRAC.**

Practicing

- Practice constant repetition.
- Make attempts to imitate a native speaker's accent.
- Concentrate on sounds.
- Practice in a realistic setting.

Receiving and Sending Messages

- Skim information to determine "need to know" vs. "nice to know."
- Use available resources (print and non-print) to interpret messages.

Analyzing and Reasoning

- Use general rules to understand the meaning.
- Work into specifics.
- Break down unfamiliar expressions into parts.

Creating Structure for Input and Output

- Choose a format for taking meaningful notes.
- Practice summarizing long passages.
- Use highlighters to emphasize main ideas or important specific details.

Metacognitive Strategies

The ESOL teacher is responsible for helping students become metacognitive—that is, the teacher tries to help students to become aware of their own individual learning strategies in order to constantly improve those strategies and add to them. Each student should have his or her own "toolbox" of skills for centering, planning, managing, and evaluating the language-learning process.

Centering Learning

- Review a key concept or principle and link it to already existing knowledge.
- Make a firm decision to pay attention to the general concept.
- Ignore input that is distracting.
- Learn skills in the proper order.

Arranging and Planning Learning

- Take the time to understand how a language is learned.
- Create optimal learning conditions (regulate noise, lighting, temperature, etc.).
- Obtain the appropriate books and other resources.
- Set reasonable short- and long-term goals.

Evaluating Learning

- Keep track of errors that prevent further progress.
- Keep track of progress (e.g., the student reads faster now than the student could the previous month).

Socioaffective Strategies

Socioaffective strategies include affective and social strategies.

Affective Strategies

Affective strategies are those that the learner can use to control the emotions and attitudes that hinder progress in learning the second language, and at the same time learn to interact in a social environment.

There are three sets of affective strategies: lowering anxiety, encouragement, and taking emotional temperature. These are easily remembered with the acronym **LET.**

- **Lowering anxiety:** These strategies help the learner maintain emotional equilibrium with physical activities. Use meditation and/or deep breathing to relax, listen to calming music, read a funny book, or watch a comedy.

- **Encouragement:** These strategies help support and self-motivate the learner. Stay positive through self-affirmations, take risks, and give rewards.

- **Taking emotional temperature:** These strategies help learners control their emotions by understanding what they are feeling, as well as why they are feeling that way. Listen to body signals; create a checklist to keep track of feelings and motivations during the second-language acquisition process; keep a diary to record progress and feelings; and share feelings with a classmate or friend.

Social Strategies

Social strategies help the learner interact in social settings. The following are three useful strategies for interacting socially: asking questions, cooperating with others, and empathizing with others. These can be remembered by the acronym **ACE.**

- **Asking questions:** Ask for clarification or help. Request that the speaker slow down, repeat, or paraphrase and ask to be corrected.

- **Cooperating with others:** Interact with more than one person: work cooperatively with a partner or small group, and work with a native speaker of the language.

- **Empathizing with others:** Learn to relate to others, remembering that people usually have more aspects in common than differences. Empathize with another student by learning about his or her culture and by being aware of and sensitive to the thoughts and feelings of others. For example, perhaps a fellow student is sad because of something that has happened. Understanding and empathizing will help that student, and it will also help the empathizer.

SKILL 2.4   **Analyze the interrelatedness of first- and second-language acquisition and ways in which L1 may affect development of L2**

Barring physical disabilities or isolation from other humans, language is universal. Developing language is a lifelong process in one's native language, and one must go through similar processes to thoroughly acquire or learn a foreign language.

First-Language Skills

Many studies have found that cognitive and academic development in the first language has an extremely important and positive effect on second-language schooling (e.g., Bialystok, 1991; Collier, 1989, 1992; Garcia, 2001; Genesee, 1987, 1994; Thomas & Collier, 1995). It is, therefore, important that language learners continue to develop their first-language skills because the most gifted 5-year-old is approximately halfway through the process of first-language development. From the ages of 6 to 12, the child continues to acquire subtle phonological distinctions, vocabulary, semantics, syntax, formal discourse patterns, and the complexities of pragmatics in the oral system of his or her first language (Berko Gleason, 1993).

These skills can be transferred to acquiring or learning a second language. When ELLs already know how to read and write in their first language, they can transfer many of their primary language skills to their target language. They have already learned the relationship between print and spoken language, that print can be used for many different things, and that writing conveys messages from its author. Grellet (1981) has stated that the knowledge "one brings to the text is often more important than what one finds in it."

Teachers can build on this previous knowledge and address specifics in English as they arise.

The Use of Interlanguage

Interlanguage is a strategy used by a second-language learner to compensate for his or her lack of proficiency while learning the second language. It cannot be classified as L1, nor can it be classified as L2; rather it could almost be considered an L3, complete with its own grammar and lexicon. Interlanguage is developed by the learner in relation to the learner's experiences (both positive and negative) with the second language. Larry Selinker introduced the theory of interlanguage and asserted that L2 learners create certain learning strategies to compensate during this in-between period of acquiring the second language. These practices create an interlanguage, which assists the learner in moving from one stage to the next during second-language acquisition.

- **Overgeneralization** occurs when the learner attempts to apply a rule across the board, without regard to irregular exceptions. For example, a learner is overgeneralizing when he or she attempts to apply an "ed" to create a past tense for an irregular verb, such as "buyed" or "swimmed."

- **Simplification** refers to the L2 learner using resources that require limited vocabulary to aid comprehension and allow the learner to listen, read, and speak in the target language at a very elementary level. This practice involves modifying language to facilitate comprehension. Researchers disagree on the value of this practice. Krashen believes that simplification aids L2 acquisition. Others believe that lessening authentic texts diminishes L2 learners' ability to comprehend more difficult texts.

- **L1 interference** or **language transfer** occurs when a learner's primary language influences his or her progress in the L2. Interference most commonly affects pronunciation, grammar structures, vocabulary, and semantics.

Selinker theorizes that a psychological structure is awakened when a learner begins the process of second-language acquisition. He attaches great significance to the notion that the learner and the native speaker will not create similar sounds if they attempt to communicate the same thought, idea, or meaning.

Fossilization is a term applied by Selinker to the process in which an L1 learner reaches a plateau and accepts that less than fluent level, which prevents the learner from achieving L2 fluency. Fossilization occurs when non-L1 forms become fixed in the interlanguage of the L2 learner. L2 learners are highly susceptible to this phenomenon during the early stages.

SKILL 2.5   **Know common difficulties and effective strategies to help students overcome those difficulties.**

Research demonstrates that language learners acquire (or learn) language when they are ready to process it. According to different theories, a student's interlanguage is the language a student develops that is somewhere between L1 and L2. The interlanguage can be visualized as a midpoint on a continuum between L1 and L2 or may be represented by a Venn diagram. This interlanguage changes as the ELL learns more of the L2 structure and approaches native-language fluency.

Language is not acquired lineally, but is influenced by individual factors such as age, personality, educational background, previous L1 and L2 language experience, and context. Contradictions in second-language learning may be explained by Long's (1990) **backsliding theory** or the so-called **U-shaped behavior.** Larsen-Freeman (1997) refers to this period as a period of randomness and suggests that the Chaos theory is the most satisfactory theory for the seemingly unstable system of second-language learning.

Presentation, Practice, and Production

Teachers often follow the **Presentation, Practice, Production (PPP)** model. In this model, teachers take the following steps to help English language learners acquire communication (production):

- Present small amounts of language
- Give the ELLs the opportunity to practice the items
- Integrate the items into the other language

The last step involves repetition. Items should be retaught and recycled at frequent intervals for the ELLs to firmly acquire the needed language items and make them a solid part of their language skills.

Idioms

Idioms present a particular challenge to ELLs. Here, again, creating contexts facilitates learning. Grouping idioms according to types of language use helps. Some idioms rely on synonyms, some hyperbole, others metaphor.

Most idioms do not translate into another language with the same meaning and the same type of wordplay, especially in Spanish. However, each language does have its own set of idioms. Having students generate a list of idioms in their native language will strengthen their ability to understand and appreciate idioms in English. Also, having students create their own original idioms increases understanding.

How idioms are taught greatly affects how well they are remembered and the level of frustration the ELL experiences. Visual representations of idioms make meaning easier to understand and provide a memory cue to prompt recall. Using commercially produced illustrations or having students draw their own representation of the meaning makes learning idioms easier and more fun. Students can also write stories or perform skits that illustrate the meaning of idioms.

DOMAIN II   ESL INSTRUCTION AND ASSESSMENT

COMPETENCY 3

THE ESL TEACHER UNDERSTANDS ESL TEACHING METHODS AND USES THIS KNOWLEDGE TO PLAN AND IMPLEMENT EFFECTIVE, DEVELOPMENTALLY APPROPRIATE INSTRUCTION

SKILL 3.1   Know applicable Texas Essential Knowledge and Skills (TEKS) and the English Language Proficiency Standards (ELPS), and know how to design and implement appropriate instruction to address the domains of listening, speaking, reading, and writing

State Standards

The **Texas Essential Knowledge and Skills (TEKS)** are the state standards for Texas K-12 education in public schools. The **English Language Proficiency Standards (ELPS)** provide descriptors of the levels used to determine ELLs' English language proficiency. School districts are required to implement ELPS for each subject in the required curriculum. The ELPS are used to determine a student's cross-curricular second-language acquisition. The standards include

- **Learning strategies standards:** ELLs use language-learning strategies to develop an awareness of his or her own learning processes in all content areas.

- **K-12 listening standards:** ELLs listen to a variety of speakers and electronic media to gain an increasing level of comprehension of acquired language in all content areas.

- **K-12 speaking standards:** ELLs speak for a variety of purposes while recognizing different language registers (formal/informal), using vocabulary with increasing fluency and accuracy in language arts and all content areas.

- **2–12 reading standards:** ELLs read a variety of texts with an increasing level of comprehension in all content areas.

- **2–12 writing standards:** ELLs write with increasing accuracy for a specific purpose and audience in all content areas.

Within each standard are levels of proficiency: beginning, intermediate, advanced, and advanced high. The proficiency levels are not grade-specific. ELLs may well exhibit different proficiency levels within each domain, or standard. The descriptor for each level progresses from one level to the next and provides information for educators to determine where a student is with language acquisition. These standards and levels of proficiency are also used as a measurement tool in the **Texas English Language Proficiency Assessment System (TELPAS),** an exam that tests the proficiency level of each ELL. For more information on the ELPS, see Skill 7.5.

The following website details the English Language Proficiency Standards: http://portal.esc20.net/portal/page/portal/esc20public/ELPS_EnglishLanguageProficiency Standards.

For details on the Texas English Language and Arts curriculum, visit http://ritter.tea.state.tx.us/rules/tac/chapter110/.

Instructional Design

Research in the area of instructional design and implementation has come up with useful insights that can be applied across both grade level and language classroom settings in order to support ESL students' English language and literacy development. Language and literacy development are the key objectives of any grade-level curriculum to ensure success both inside and outside the school setting.

These insights can be synthesized into seven key instructional criteria for designing and conducting instruction to support ESL students' language and literacy development (Enright, 1991).

1. **Collaboration:** Instruction is organized so that students have many opportunities to interact and work cooperatively with each other and with teachers, family members, and community members. During collaborative activities in the classroom, teachers and students actively work together in order for learning to take place. Collaborative instruction entails activities that require communicating and sharing, such as discussion groups, student partners, or student-teacher dialogue journals. Collaborative activities may also involve students in interacting with people outside of the classroom, such as interviewing the school drama club for the class newspaper or working with a parent or an elder regarding special family traditions.

2. **Purpose:** Instruction is organized so that students have multiple opportunities to use authentic oral and written language to complete tasks for real-life goals and purposes. An example of purposeful composition and questioning activities would be students writing letters to city officials to invite them to a class election forum and then interviewing them about school issues. In addition to this, there are four major kinds of purposeful discourse that can be used as part of learning activities across the curriculum. These are (a) **shared discourse,** in which language is used socially to communicate and share meaning in order to accomplish social goals (playing games or planning a short scene); (b) **fun discourse,** in which language is used for fun (singing songs and writing riddles); (c) **fact discourse,** in which

language is used to get new information and concepts (doing a research project); and (d) **thought discourse,** in which language is used to imagine and create new ideas and experiences (writing poetry or critical thinking). These discourse features ensure that students learn both language and content with clear goals in mind.

3. **Student interest:** Instruction is organized to both promote and follow students' interest. This does not mean that the instructional goals are changed, but the focus is on organizing activities which combine students' interests and purposes with the curriculum topics and objectives.

4. **Previous experience:** Instruction is organized to include students' previous experiences in the new learning. This includes tapping students' previous language and literacy experiences in their first language and English, and also their already-developed knowledge and cultural experiences. This type of activity entails relating new concepts and materials to students' background experiences, such as brainstorming ideas before reading a text or connecting previous class activities to new ones. An example would be including histories and folktales from ESL students' families and native countries in reading-group instruction, or having students collect authentic speech and literacy data from their homes and neighborhoods and discussing their findings in class.

5. **Support:** Instruction is organized so that students feel comfortable and take risks when using English. The classroom atmosphere should be supportive, providing challenging but safe opportunities for students to learn English. The activities are adapted to students' current language and literacy capabilities or **zones of proximal development** (Vygotsky, 1978) in the second language, providing scaffolding of the newly acquired skills.

6. **Variety:** Instruction is organized to include a variety of learning activities and language forms and uses. Variety means that students are exposed to a wide range of oral and written English that they are expected to use in classrooms and in their daily lives. The organization of variety includes the instructional practices of collaboration, defining learning purposes, incorporating student interests, and providing familiar and unfamiliar student experiences within classroom learning activities.

7. **Integration:** Instruction is organized to integrate the various programs and resources available for supporting ELLs' language and literacy development so that they complement each other. This may include integrating the students' in-school and out-of-school experiences; integrating content and language instruction; integrating the four language skills of reading, writing, listening, and speaking; and integrating the students within the classroom through cooperative learning.

SKILL 3.2   **Know effective instructional methods and techniques for the ESL classroom, and select and use instructional methods, resources, and materials appropriate for addressing specified instructional goals and promoting learning in students with diverse characteristics and needs**

Curriculum objectives are based on the needs and backgrounds of the students. The needs of students learning English as an additional language have resulted in an increasing demand on all teachers, including both content and language teachers, to adapt their methods to meet these needs.

Teacher Discourse

Enright (1991) puts forward modifications in "teacher talk" that could help make language accessible to students. Krashen and Terrell (1983) refer to it as comprehensible input, meaning discourse that is just beyond ESOL students' current language capabilities. There are various ways in which language teachers and content area teachers can adapt their own classroom discourse to make it comprehensible and useful:

- **Nonverbal adaptations:** Teachers use gestures, nonverbal illustrations of meanings, and facial expressions.

- **Contextual adaptations:** Teachers use visual aids (e.g., pictures, blackboard sketches, real-life objects) and auditory aids (e.g., recorded sounds or recorded speech).

- **Paraverbal adaptations:** Teachers speak more clearly, slowing down the rate of their speech, and pausing between major idea units, varying their volume and intonation to convey meaning.

- **Discourse adaptations:** Teachers use organizational markers, such as "now" and "first," to make their discourse more comprehensible. They also rephrase their utterances and repeat their utterances in meaningful ways.

- **Elicitation adaptations:** Teachers use a variety of techniques to call on students to ensure student involvement. For example, they call on students by name, they call for volunteers to respond, they call on the whole group, and they have open elicitations allowing anyone to speak.

- **Questioning adaptations:** Teachers vary their questions according to the proficiency level of the students. For students with limited English proficiency, the answer could be a drawing, an action, or a one-word response. Required responses can become more complicated as the proficiency level progresses.

- **Response adaptations:** Teachers adapt their responses to students' utterances to provide further comprehensible input and to encourage further language use by providing *confirmation checks* and *clarification requests*. Teachers rephrase students' responses to provide further information on the topic. Teachers encourage students' responses by giving them more *wait time* between the question and the response, by *prompting,* and by *repeating* the response.

- **Correction adaptations:** Teachers correct students' responses by focusing on the meaning conveyed, by modeling the correct answer, or by explicitly showing the student his or her error and providing corrective feedback individually or away from the group.

These modifications to teacher discourse are beneficial, but it is important that teacher talk does not dominate class discourse. Learning activities should focus on student collaboration in pairs and groups, and independent work. This variety allows students to receive more comprehensible input from many sources and to use it in many ways.

Collier emphasizes that students who do not reach a threshold of knowledge in their first language, including literacy, may experience cognitive difficulties in their second language (Collier, 1995; Thomas & Collier, 1995). The continued development of uninterrupted cognitive development is key. It is a disservice to parents and children to encourage the use of second language instead of first language at home, precisely because both are working at a level below their actual cognitive maturity. Whereas nonnative speakers in kindergarten through second or third grade may do well if schooled in English part or all of the day, from fourth grade through high school, students with little or no academic or cognitive development in their first language do less and less well as they move into the upper grades where academic and cognitive demands are greater (Collier, 1995).

Printed and Electronic Texts

The text itself is a resource that may or may not increase comprehension depending on how it is written. In general, texts that have long sentences and more advanced words are more complex than texts with short, simple sentence structures and basic vocabulary words. For ELLs, it may be necessary to obtain basic readers to help them overcome cognitive difficulties.

Sometimes texts are difficult to understand because they discuss topics not familiar to the reader. When the student's prior knowledge or background knowledge is activated, the ELL is able to attach meaning to new information by joining the new with the old to achieve comprehension. Children who come from backgrounds in which reading was not possible or who did not attend a preschool program may be at a disadvantage when entering a mainstream kindergarten or school reading program.

Texts may be difficult for beginning readers because they are not user-friendly. Texts that highlight new vocabulary, summarize key points, and contain introductions and summaries include features that will help the struggling reader.

According to Vygotsky (1978), the sociocultural context from which a student comes is crucial. The community, home, school, and classroom contexts exert influence on the performance of an individual student or a group of students. Students who have been classified as low achievers in reading may resent the stigma and continue to perform poorly or react negatively to assessment.

Atkinson and Hansen (1966–67) published the first study of the use of computers in reading instruction. Students at Stanford University accessed reading lessons similar to traditional worksheets on a mainframe computer. Today, the computer is used in all aspects of our lives, and the large majority of today's students will experience some form of computer learning.

Blanton and Menendez (in Schumm, 2006) mention seven categories discussing how computers are used in reading instruction:

- **Game applications,** such as *Reader Rabbit, Missing Link,* and *Reading Blaster*

- **General applications,** such as Microsoft Word, PowerPoint, HyperStudio, Kid Pix, and Storybook Weaver

- **Access applications**, such as Google, Netscape, and Yahooligans!

- **Tutoring applications,** such as *Watch Me Read*

- **Thinking and problem-solving applications,** such as *Oregon Trail, SimCity, SimEarth,* and *Zoombinis Island Odyssey*

- **Communication applications,** such as email and online discussion spaces

- **Integrated learning systems (ILS),** such as the Waterford *Early Reading Program, Fast ForWord,* and *Read 180*

Graphic Organizers

Graphic organizers are frameworks that help students visualize raw data. These can be used by the teacher for simplification of complex materials, numerous data, and complicated relationships in content areas. Students learn to analyze data, organize information, and clarify concepts. Examples are pie charts, flowcharts, bar graphs, Venn diagrams, family trees, spider maps, organizational charts, and strip maps. Still other graphic organizers are webbing, concept mapping, passwords and language ladders, and brainstorming.

- With **webbing**, students learn to associate words or phrases with a topic or concept.

- By using **concept maps**, students learn the relationships between the different elements of a topic and how to organize them from the most general to the most specific. This is different from webbing, in which relationships between words or phrases are shown but not ranked.

- **Passwords** and **language ladders** are motivating ways to teach chunks of language to ELLs. The "password" of the day is language needed for daily student life in school. After the words or phrases are explained, they are posted on the board and must be used before leaving the room or participating in some activity. Language ladders are associated words such as different ways to say "hello" or "good-bye."

- **Brainstorming** consists of students contributing ideas related to a concept or problem-centered topic. The teacher initially accepts all ideas without comment. Students then categorize, prioritize, and select proposed selections for further investigation.

For more information on graphic organizers, see Skill 6.2.

Classroom Strategies

Moll (1988) discusses the value of the funds of knowledge that students bring to the classroom. These resources are made up of students' prior knowledge that can be tapped through **daily journal writings.** The knowledge gained regarding students' lives can be incorporated into lessons and content for coursework. It also helps in choosing topics that would be of interest to students, thereby engaging them in the learning process. For example, a teacher can plan a unit in which students pick an area of the city they want to learn more about. Students research their selected topic and then prepare a report or a project. Parents and family members can help students and become part of this research.

Saunders and Goldenberg (1999) and Echevarria (1995) presented an interactive form of initiation and feedback called **instructional conversations (IC).** The purpose of IC is to create a comfortable and safe atmosphere for the students to express ideas without holding back. In this approach, students engage in extended conversations with teachers and with each other to promote language development. For example, the teacher will say, "Tell me more about . . . " and "What do you mean by . . . " and will restate students' comments, "In other words. . . . "

It has also been found that teachers who speak with clarity, use gestures, controlled vocabulary, and cognates, preteach difficult vocabulary, and tap students' prior knowledge are most successful.

Pairs and group activities are important ways in which students can participate and feel valued. In such groupings, students of different cultural and academic backgrounds work together and participate actively. In addition, teachers can, at times, pair individuals with different strengths, so that students can learn from each other. This increases the comfort level of the students, especially quiet students and those who are struggling with English. Cooperative grouping gives opportunities for students to share ideas and information, which promotes problem solving.

Graves (2012) observes that teachers who seem to know each of their students and who take an active interest in them are most successful. Teachers should be in contact with the parents and involve them in their children's learning.

Teachers should also model for their students how to think through problems and acknowledge the difficulty of the language acquisition process. It helps students to see how teachers think aloud to express their own thoughts, attitudes, feelings, and learning strategies (Brown, 2008). This **modeling of learning strategies** by experts can show students the processes that underlie expert performance. This modeling can also be done by peers or student tutors, making the goals seem more achievable for the students.

In addition to modeling, teachers should plan instruction so that students can experience success and develop independent learning skills. This process is referred to as scaffolding: the teacher initially provides sufficient support to practice newly acquired skills and experiment with new concepts until those concepts and skills are clear and become part of the learning process (see Skill 3.3).

Multiple Intelligences

Teachers need to be aware of the different ways in which students learn, so that they can prepare classroom experiences and materials that encompass the different learning styles. Teachers should use multiple-intelligence approaches to teaching the same lesson. Humans learn in at least seven different ways: visually/spatially, musically, verbally, logically/mathematically, interpersonally, intrapersonally, and bodily/kinesthetically (Gardner, 1999). These factors should be kept in mind when planning a lesson.

ELLs can benefit from a variety of instructional methods that cater to different learning styles. For example, the tactile learner can perform hands-on activities, increasing the student's learning experience. During such activities, students learn while discussing, investigating, creating, and discovering with other students. In time, students gain background regarding the subject they are learning and start making their own decisions, requiring less teacher support and more student-centered interactions (Cooperstein & Kocevar-Weidinger, 2004).

According to Cassidy (2004), the holistic-analytical dimension concerns the way in which individuals tend to process information, either as a whole (holistic) or broken down into parts (analytic). Riding and Cheema (1991: in Cassidy, 2004) determined that the holistic-analytical learner is commonly associated with the following terms: analytic-deductive, rigorous, constrained, convergent, formal, critical, and synthetic. The verbalizer-imager dimension concerns the way in which individuals tend to represent information either as words or as images (Cassidy, 2004).

SKILL 3.3   **Apply knowledge of effective practices, resources, and materials for providing content-based ESL instruction, engaging students in critical thinking, and fostering students' communicative competence**

Creating effective ESL instruction involves applying knowledge of the practices, resources, and materials (many of which were discussed in Skill 3.2) to the specific needs of the students.

Scaffolding

Scaffolding, or supporting, children of all ages consists of demonstrating, guiding, and teaching in a step-by-step process while ELLs are trying to communicate effectively and develop their language skills (Cazden,1983; Ninio & Bruner, 1988). The amount of scaffolding depends on the support needed and the individual child. It allows the ELL to assume more and more responsibility as he or she is able. Once the ELLs feel secure in their abilities, they are ready to move on to the next stage.

Educational scaffolding consists of several linked strategies, including modeling academic language and contextualizing academic language, using visuals, gestures, and demonstrations to help students while they are involved in hands-on learning. ESL teachers provide much of the scaffolding by observing and providing feedback while students work in groups or pairs (Zwiers & Crawford, 2011). Some efficient scaffolding techniques are providing direction, clarifying purpose, keeping the student on task with proposed rubrics that clarify expectations, offering suggestions for resources, and supplying a lesson or activity without problems.

Tompkins (2009) identified five levels of scaffolding for learning and problem solving to show how ELLs moved from needing considerable support, to the independent level where they were ready to solve problems on their own.

- **Modeling:** The instructor models orally or through written supports (a paragraph, a paper, an example) the work expected of the ELL. Projects from previous years can provide examples of the type of work expected.

- **Shared:** ELLs use their pooled knowledge of the project (and that of their teacher) to complete the assignment.

- **Interactive:** The teacher allows ELLs to question him or her on points that need clarification or are not understood (i.e., everyone is a learner). It is especially satisfying for the student when the teacher admits that she does not know the answer and helps the students locate it.

- **Guided:** Well-posed questions, clues, reminders, and examples are all ways of guiding the ELL toward the goal.

- **Independent levels:** The learner achieves independence and no longer needs educational scaffolding.

Making Material Comprehensible to ELLs

In addition to scaffolding, other techniques can be used successfully to adapt materials for ELLs. Facial expressions and gestures help ELLs understand materials that may be at their instruction level–that is, just above their level of understanding (what Krashen calls $i + 1$). Both of these techniques can be overused and limit student learning if the ELLs are not sufficiently challenged academically.

Classroom materials have various difficulty levels. Teachers make the material comprehensible to the students when they guide the ELLs through the story. They can provide graphic organizers so that students learn to analyze the materials presented to them in a way that helps them to visualize the main points and the connections among them.

Questions such as *What can we learn from this? How can we do this in real life? How are people like this?* are part of the teacher's repertoire but are especially important when dealing with ELLs who may not be able to see how the text relates to their lives nor incorporate the message or meaning unless led by clever questions. For history, questions would include *Why? Where? What happened?* and summarizing by *Therefore. . . .* Other content areas have their own vocabulary and language conventions, and teachers must directly teach these for the ELLs to become successful in each content area.

Creating a Relaxed Classroom Environment

To enhance communicative competence, it is paramount to provide students with a relaxed classroom environment in which they feel comfortable and confident. A relaxed atmosphere allows the students to take risks and feel confident to interact further. The teacher should also provide the students with sufficient opportunities to speak in situations as close as possible to real life. The speakers' focus is on the communicative task itself, for which they collaborate to achieve mutual understanding and modify their language according to the demands of the situation.

Interactive group work is also important to lessen students' anxiety and lower their affective filters. Different group sizes (pairs, small groups, and large groups) provide opportunities for students to practice the different thinking and oral skills that are unique to each group type. When students' affective filter is lowered, they are more likely to take risks and engage in more meaningful conversations without the fear of mistakes. Students also develop social skills by interacting in a variety of small group situations that aim to resolve a problem, give directions or advice, and so on.

In these classrooms, the teacher and the students are co-learners whose goal is to communicate meaningful ideas and information. The teacher builds on what the students already know, which helps them expand on their prior knowledge and retain information. The questions asked in the class should produce a variety of responses for which there is no right answer. Furthermore, students should be provided with ample opportunities for comprehensible input where meaning is negotiated within a meaningful context. Some strategies for a communicative classroom could be peer interviews, problem-solving conversations, debates, and so on.

Additionally, it is important to provide students with comprehensible input. For instance, for beginning-level ESL students, comprehensible input would be in the form of short sentences, phrases, and relatively simple language segments that are integrated into activities of purposeful communication. Similarly, second-language learners should communicate in situations or exchanges that are as authentic as possible and should bring about a maximum of personal involvement in the communication. Students should also be provided opportunities to use the target language in social interactions that allow the student to produce the language in a particular context.

SKILL 3.4 Know how to integrate technological tools and resources into instructional practice to facilitate and enhance student learning

The tools teachers have available to them to present information to students are always increasing. Not long ago, teachers only needed to know how to use word-processing programs, grading programs, and overhead projectors. Today, electronic slideshows are standard, and other methods of information distribution, such as Web blogs, are expected by principals, parents, and students alike.

Integrating Technology into the ESL Classroom

Educational technology can increase learning opportunities for ELLs. Developing effective and adequate strategies is crucial to integrating technology in multiple ways into the ESL classroom. Competent use of computers prevents ELLs from "academic and social marginalization" (Murray & Kouritzin, 1997: 187). It allows them to have the most control over the direction of their learning by controlling their time, speed of learning, autonomy, choice of topics, or even their own identity (Hoven, 1992). Technology gives prompt feedback, individualizes learning, and tailors the instructional sequence. It can meet specific student needs, increase autonomy, allow for more responsibility, promote equal opportunities in a nonsexist environment, foster student cooperation with peers, and encourage students to make decisions (Burgess & Trinidad, 1997).

Tools such as email, databases, spreadsheets, and word processors can help enhance ELLs' English skills—and, if necessary, build on their native language skills—through the availability of online dictionaries or spellcheckers (Johns & Tórrez, 2001). Technology has evolved from its support function to play a role in initiating learning processes. It can provide a flexible learning environment where students can really explore and be engaged. Hypermedia, for example, individually addresses levels of fluency, content knowledge, student motivation, and interest, allowing inclusion of English language students, who can thus monitor their comprehension, language production, and behavior (Bermudez & Palumbo, 1994).

Technology integration defined by Reilly (2002) is curriculum development. It is one way to move teaching from a teacher- to a learner-centered approach. To allow for greater success rates for ELLs, teachers need to integrate technology to advance student learning because technology activities, such as using the Internet or working as a team on a project, provide students with opportunities to enhance and extend regular learning to higher levels of cognitive involvement. The effect of engaging ELLs through technology can be multilayered. When technology is used as part of a model that involves students in complex authentic tasks, the results can be student-centered cooperative learning, increased teacher-student and peer interaction, and more positive attitudes toward learning, allowing greater interaction and sense of responsibility to a team.

Internet and software can enrich the learning process whereby students can look up images and other content-area information. These activities can accelerate content learning by addressing relevant information and are not solely dependent on reading English. Through experiences such as these, ELLs have opportunities to participate in an engaging learning environment and learn at higher levels of cognition. With technology, these students can control and self-direct their learning and get immediate feedback. They no longer depend on direct teacher instruction that often limits the student to passive listening and watching the teacher. While direct teacher control is evidently lower in technology-based classrooms (e.g., a computer lab), the instruction is ever more demanding on the teacher. The teacher becomes a facilitator, rather than a "deliverer or transmitter of knowledge" (Padrón & Waxman, 1996: 348). Teachers scaffold their students' learning experiences to build high-quality instruction.

The following are some activities using technology that are intended to support learner knowledge construction:

- Online collaboration with classrooms around the world
- Education applications of the Web such as email exchanges, online bulletin boards, and information searching
- Use of multimedia to create projects (Hartley & Bendixen, 2001)

When students are engaged in activities like these, they are constructing their own knowledge, with the teacher as facilitator of the process.

Incorporating technology effectively into a fully content- and skill-based curriculum requires a good understanding of lesson objectives and how those objectives can be met with the technology. While teachers should definitely consider technological integration as an important aspect of their work in any subject and at any grade level, teachers should not include technology simply for the sake of technology. The best approach, considering that all subjects can in certain ways be enhanced with technology, is for the teacher to consider a variety of lessons and units and decide which focus areas can be enhanced with technological tools. Both teacher and learner need to be aware of their own learning styles and strategies as well (Hoven, 2006).

Finally, it is important to remember that, as with all other learning, technological learning must be developmentally appropriate. Although very young students can perform various functions on the computer, by virtue of development level the time required for a particular activity may be greatly increased. Furthermore, various technological tools are simply too advanced, too fast, and too complex for very young students. It may be best to introduce basic elements of technology in the earlier grades.

Using the Internet

The Internet is a tool and, as such, should be used with an instructional purpose in mind. Instructors should ask themselves if the Internet is the most efficient and effective medium to reach the instructional goals. The following guidelines will help in determining the value of such projects:

- Assign projects that are meaningful, well designed, and interesting to students.
- Use the Internet is a tool and not a means in itself.
- Make sure projects have specific goals and are timely.
- Start small until you gain experience in planning telecommunications projects.
- Communicate frequently (at least once a week) with all participants.
- Share the results with the participants, the school, and the community.

Two valuable resources for ESOL teachers are WebQuests and electronic portfolios. By using these tools, teachers are able to create their own projects based on established criteria.

WebQuests were developed by Bernie Dodge of San Diego State University. They allow students to work independently or in small groups while doing research, problem solving, and applying basic skills. The essential components of WebQuests are Introduction, Task, Process, Resources, Evaluation, and Conclusion.

An **electronic portfolio** is a concise, annotated collection of a student's work that displays his or her knowledge, understanding, skills, accomplishments, interests, and achievements over a period of time. By placing this information on the Web, a CD, or a flash drive, students communicate with teachers, parents, and others about their learning. The key elements of an electronic portfolio are deciding on goals; designing flowcharts, storyboards, and templates needed for the portfolio; developing the multimedia elements needed and creating the portfolio; and evaluating the product and the process.

SKILL 3.5 Apply effective classroom management and teaching strategies for a variety of ESL environments and situations

All students need to understand and follow classroom rules from the very beginning, and ELLs are no exception. Teach them classroom management rules as soon as possible to avoid misunderstandings, discipline problems, and feelings of low self-esteem. The following are a few strategies that can be used in class:

- Use visuals, like pictures and symbols, and reward systems to communicate expectations in a positive and direct manner.

- Physically model language to ELLs in classroom routines and instructional activities. ELLs will need to see teachers or peers model behavior when they are asked to sit down, walk to the bulletin board, work with a partner, copy a word, and so on.

- Be consistent and fair with all students. Once ELLs clearly understand what is expected, hold them equally accountable for their behavior.

Classroom Management Plans

Classroom management plans should be in place when the school year begins. Developing a management plan requires a proactive approach. A proactive approach involves deciding what behaviors will be expected of the class as a whole, anticipating possible problems, teaching the behaviors early in the school year, and implementing behavior management techniques that focus on positive procedures that can be used at home as well at school. It is important to involve the students in the development of classroom rules. The benefits include the following:

- Students understand the rationale for the rules.
- Students assume responsibility for following the rules because they had a part in developing them.

Once rules are established, enforcement and reinforcement for following the rules should begin right away.

Consequences should be introduced when rules are introduced, clearly stated, and understood by all students. The severity of the consequence should match the severity of the offense and must be enforceable. The teacher must apply the consequence consistently and fairly, so students will know what to expect when they choose to break a rule.

Like consequences, students should understand what rewards to expect for following the rules. The teacher should never promise a reward that cannot be delivered, and should follow through with the reward as soon as possible. Consistency and fairness are necessary for rewards to be effective. Students will become frustrated and give up if they see that rewards and consequences are not delivered in a fair and timely way. In the absence of effective school-wide and classroom management systems, quality instruction and focused learning cannot occur.

Helping ELLs Feel Welcome in the Classroom

Although there are no specific teaching techniques to make ELLs feel that they belong in a new culture, there are ways to make them feel welcome in the classroom.

- **Learn their names:** Take the time to learn how to pronounce each English language learner's name correctly. Ask them to say their names. Listen carefully and repeat them. In addition to learning the ELLs' names well, model the correct pronunciation of their names to the class so that all students can pronounce them correctly.

- **Offer one-on-one assistance when possible:** Some ELLs may not answer voluntarily in class or ask for help even if they need it. ELLs may smile and nod, but this does not necessarily mean that they understand. Individual coaching can be offered in a friendly way. It may be helpful to seat ELLs near the teacher's desk.

- **Assign a peer partner:** Teachers should choose a classmate who really wants to help an ELL as a peer. This student can make sure that the ELL understands what he or she is supposed to do. It will be even more helpful if the peer partner knows the ELL's first language.

- **Post a visual daily schedule:** Even if ELLs do not understand all the words that teachers speak, it is possible for them to understand the structure of each day. Whether through chalkboard art or images on Velcro®, teachers can post the daily schedule each morning. By writing down times and having pictures next to words like lunch, wash hands, math, and field trip, ELLs can have a general sense of the upcoming day.

- **Use materials related to your ELLs' cultures:** Students respond when they see books, topics, characters, and images that are familiar. Try to achieve a good balance of books and materials that include different cultures.

- **Include ELLs in a nonthreatening manner:** Some ELLs may be apprehensive about speaking out in a group. They may be afraid to make mistakes in front of their peers. Their silence could also be a sign of respect for a teacher as an authority—not a sign of their inability or refusal to participate. Find ways to involve English language learners in a nonthreatening manner, including such techniques as Total Physical Response (see Skill 4.1) and cooperative learning projects.

- **Involve ELLs in cooperative learning:** Some ELLs are used to working cooperatively on assigned tasks. What may look like cheating is actually a culturally acquired learning style—an attempt to mimic, see, or model what has to be done. Teachers can use this cultural trait in their classrooms. Assign buddies or peer tutors so that ELLs are able to participate in all class activities.

COMPETENCY 4

THE ESL TEACHER UNDERSTANDS HOW TO PROMOTE STUDENTS' COMMUNICATIVE LANGUAGE DEVELOPMENT IN ENGLISH

SKILL 4.1   **Know applicable Texas Essential Knowledge and Skills (TEKS), especially the English language arts and reading curriculum as it relates to ESL, and know how to design and implement appropriate instruction to address TEKS (i.e., listening, speaking, reading, writing, viewing/representing)**

The following website details the Texas English language arts curriculum: http://ritter.tea.state.tx.us/rules/tac/chapter110/.

Structured Language-Building Tasks

Some activities that teachers can do to encourage more oral production from ELLs in authentic situations are the following:

- **Total Physical Response (TPR):** Give commands to which students must respond to show understanding. The children's game "Simon Says" may be used with students of all ages by increasing the stakes (e.g., Give commands at a faster rate or make them more complex, always keeping in mind the ability level of the ELLs).

- **Group work:** Encourage authentic language by structuring tasks when ELLs ask for clarification, participate in discussions, interrupt each other, compete for the floor, and kid around. Group work also encourages learner autonomy.

- **Task-based activities:** Offer activities that require the members of the group to achieve an objective and express it in notes, rearrangement of jumbled items, a drawing, or a spoken summary.

Ellis (1994: 596–98) concluded that two-way exchanges of information show more benefits:

- Two-way tasks require more negotiation of meaning.

- ELLs usually produce more complex and accurate language when they have sufficient time to plan their responses.

- Closed tasks (those with one single, correct solution) produce more negotiation work than those without a predetermined solution.

Real-Life Listening Situations

With respect to listening skills, Ur (1996) lists some of the occasions on which we listen and appropriately respond:

- Interviews
- Instructions
- Loudspeaker announcements
- Radio news
- Committee meetings
- Shopping encounters
- Theater
- Telephone calls
- Lessons or lectures
- Conversation and gossip
- Television
- Storytelling

Most of these situations use language that is informal and spontaneous. In the classroom, teachers are training ELLs for real-life listening situations. Bearing this in mind, the most useful types of activities are those wherein the listener (the ELL) is asked to listen to genuinely informal talk instead of the typical written text. The speaker should be visible to the listener and there should be direct speaker-listener interaction. Finally, there should be only one exposure to the text, as in real life the listener will rarely have the opportunity to have the text "replayed."

The tasks themselves should be presented in such a way that the ELL can use his or her previous knowledge to anticipate outcomes. Saying, "You are going to hear a husband and wife discuss summer vacation plans" is far more useful than merely stating, "Listen to the passage. . . ." Also, ELLs should be given a task to complete as they listen (e.g., listen for information about where they are planning to go, mark this on their maps). Finally, ELLs should be permitted to answer the questions as they hear the information and not wait until the end. (Adapted from Ur, 1996)

SKILL 4.2   **Understand the role of the linguistic environment and conversational support in second-language development and use this knowledge to provide a rich, comprehensible language environment with supported opportunities for communication in English**

Interpersonal communication involves verbal and nonverbal communication. Verbal communication includes both speaking and writing; nonverbal communication includes gestures and deliberate facial expressions. Interpersonal communication is inescapable; even *not* communicating sends a message to others. It is a complicated process because of the unknowns between communicators and because language is imprecise by nature.

Communication is also contextual; sometimes, the same thing said in one context means something entirely different in another.

Teaching communication skills requires modeling by the teacher and practicing by the students. Specific skills include the following:

- **Summarizing:** A summary presents a condensed version of the original language without losing the basic meaning. Summarizing reflects understanding and the ability to break down a text or verbal exchange into its most important parts. Practicing this can be a useful tool for comprehension checks and a good preparation for taking standardized tests. Presenting a summary as a preview of a conversation or text before the ELL listens to or reads it facilitates understanding and reduces frustration.

- **Paraphrasing:** A paraphrase restates what is written or spoken. Paraphrases tend to be longer than the original text or verbal exchange without added details and attempts to explain. To paraphrase requires both comprehension and the ability to reinterpret language in much the same way that translation reproduces meaning from one language to another. For ELLs, paraphrasing increases comprehension and offers excellent vocabulary practice. Teachers or students can paraphrase parts of what is spoken or read to ensure students have understood. Paraphrasing also provides a good means to indicate listening and to affirm the speaker.

- **Listening:** Hearing what is spoken requires a more complicated process than simply hearing sounds. A variety of internal and external factors can affect understanding. ELLs must practice listening skills to avoid shutting down or misunderstanding what is said. Caution must be used to encourage active listening and avoid causing barriers. Once words are spoken, they cannot be retrieved.

- **Questioning:** Questions stimulate thinking and learning. They can be used to stimulate interest in an academic topic and to set goals for learning. Initially questions that require a one- or two-word answer should be used until learners have the skills to respond to open-ended questions. Questions can also be used to check for comprehension and to make subtle corrections. Asking good questions is a skill that requires ongoing practice. How a question is asked can either threaten or encourage the listener. Teachers should take care to model good questioning so that it encourages dialogue and does not seem like an interrogation.

- **Initiating:** In a conversation, initiating means declaring one's conversational intent and inviting consent from one's prospective conversation partner. It is a means of engaging others in interpersonal communication. Skillful initiating results in active engagement; without it, potential conversations become awkward silences.

- **Turn-taking:** Conversations progress as partners manage the flow of information back and forth between each other. By taking turns, or alternating roles of speaker and listener, ELLs develop necessary conversational skills. Without these skills, conversations come to an abrupt halt. ELLs can begin by practicing set conversations and progress to initiating and taking turns talking about topics that interest them. Formal and informal conversations must be practiced to prepare learners for the various situations they will encounter.

Communicative language competence (speaking) has been the dominant paradigm for more than two decades. Even so, it is not without its critics, who feel that the three other language skills (listening, reading, and writing), as well as other areas of the curriculum, have suffered as a consequence. For the foreseeable future, however, speaking will probably continue to be the most important skill for teachers and students alike.

McDonough and Shaw (1993: 152) enumerate our reasons for speaking as follows:

- To express ideas and opinions
- To express a wish or desire
- To negotiate and/or solve a problem
- To establish and maintain social relationships

The teacher is a fundamental source of modeling language for ELLs when the language is authentic. Yet all too often, the language between teacher and student gives little room for authentic communication, relying instead on the traditional three-part exchange: teacher's initial move, learner's response, and the teacher's follow-up move (Sinclair & Coulthard, 1975).

SKILL 4.3 Apply knowledge of practices, resources, and materials that are effective in promoting students' communicative competence in English

The teaching of speaking skills has moved away from a focus on accuracy toward a focus on fluency and communicative effectiveness. This shift has affected the kinds of activities used by the teachers in the classroom. These communicative activities promote students' abilities to understand and communicate real information. They also provide opportunities for students to engage in interaction that is closer to real-life situations.

The selection of appropriate activities depends on the level of the learners. For example, beginning ELLs need form-controlled practice and drills to move to more communicative activities. Advanced learners may be asked to engage in less structured activities on their own. Following are examples of the kinds of activities that can promote speaking skills.

Linguistically Structured Activities

Despite recent claims, a focus on accuracy is considered important for language learners. Controlled activities can be provided with a context, so that ELLs have some of the elements of a communicative activity. This approach would help the beginning-level student focus on accurate structure within a communicative context. An example is the **structured interview** in which students question and answer each other, exchanging real information while repeating and producing specific structures (e.g., yes, no, or "wh" questions).

Some language games can also provide students with controlled practice. However, it is important to model the language structures for beginning students. These and other games help students focus on and repeat specific structures as well as perform natural, "authentic" tasks.

Participation Activities

Participation activities involve students in some communication activity in a "natural" setting. One of these activities is the guided discussion, through which the teacher introduces a problem or a controversial topic. Students in small groups discuss the problem and try to come up with appropriate solutions. In more advanced classes, students could choose their own topic and lead a discussion about it. This activity advances from turn-taking elements to topic control among students, and reinforces accuracy of grammar and pronunciation. (See Skill 1.3 for more information on guided discussions.) Another activity is interviewing, wherein ELLs interview a native speaker about some meaningful or memorable experience in their lives. After the interview, the students organize the information collected and present it to the class.

Observation Activities

In observation activities, students record both verbal and nonverbal interactions between native speakers or advanced speakers of the target language. This process helps students become aware of the language spoken in an authentic setting. It also allows students to observe how people greet each other, make requests, interrupt each other, compliment each other, disagree, or receive compliments. A follow-up activity could be a role play created by students to show verbal and nonverbal behaviors appropriate in a particular situation.

Discussion Activities

Structured discussion activities allow students to work in groups or as a class to focus on a specific goal. The following are some examples.

- **Describing pictures:** Each group has a picture that all members of the group can see. A group member designated as scribe makes a check mark for each sentence the members of the group use to describe the picture. (The scribe does not have to write out the sentence.) After two minutes, the check marks are added up, and the group tries to surpass their checks by describing a second picture.

- **Picture differences:** Each pair is given a set of two pictures. Without showing their picture to their partner, they must find out what differences there are between the pictures by questioning each other.

- **Solving a problem:** Students are told that they will be on an educational advisory committee that has to advise the principal on a problem with students. They should discuss their recommendations and write a letter to the principal. (The teacher needs to prepare the problem and copy it for each student or group.)

Performance Activities

In performance activities, language learners prepare for the activity beforehand and deliver a message to a group. The activity could vary from a student's speech or explanation of an experiment to simply telling a story from their own experience. The follow-up session could involve videotaping the students during their performances and having them evaluate themselves. This activity allows students to focus on communication about their initial performance and, in the follow-up session, deal with specific language features.

Some performance activities should be chosen based on the language learner's level. For example, debates can be an effective performance activity for intermediate and advanced learners. Creative dramas and role plays can be used for all language learners, making varying demands on the learners according to their proficiency levels.

- **Creative drama:** This activity can be used in the language classroom to encourage dialogue technique. Students either write their own play or learn one from English literature. The activity is time-consuming, but increases confidence and morale of the ELLs.

- **Role plays and skits:** ELLs are each given a card describing their situation and the task or problem. The participants can be given time to practice their role play or they may improvise. This activity is usually done in pairs or small groups. (Adapted from Ur, 1996)

Communication Techniques

An ESOL instructor can use a variety of instructional methods to communicate with students. Following are some common techniques suitable for all levels.

Contextual Aids

- Gestures
- Body language
- Facial expressions

- Props
- Visual illustrations
- Manipulatives

Linguistic Modifications

- Standardized vocabulary
- Set standard for sentence length and complexity
- Reinforcement through repetition, summarization, and restatement
- Slower speaking pace

Teaching Vocabulary

- Use of charades when trying to communicate a word (acting out the word with physical actions or gestures)
- Introducing new vocabulary through familiar vocabulary (including words that have recently been studied, such as the Dolch word list)
- Utilizing visual props, antonyms, and synonyms to communicate vocabulary

As English language learners progress, these techniques are adjusted according to individual or group needs and proficiency levels.

SKILL 4.4   **Understand the interrelatedness of listening, speaking, reading, and writing, and use this knowledge to select and use effective strategies for developing students' oral language proficiency in English**

Oral language development and language skills such as reading, writing, speaking, and listening need to be developed in conjunction with one another. They are all interrelated and integrated naturally.

- **Practice** in any one area promotes development in the other areas as well.

- **Connections** between abstract and concrete concepts are best made when all language processes are incorporated and integrated during practice and application.

ELLs benefit from opportunities to use English in multiple settings. Learning is more effective when students have an opportunity to participate fully, actively discussing ideas and information.

Opportunities for Interaction

Through meaningful interaction, students can practice speaking and making themselves understood by asking and answering questions, negotiating meaning, clarifying ideas, and other techniques. These activities require the use of the four language skills (reading, writing, speaking, and listening) in order to successfully complete each task.

- Effective teachers strive to provide a more balanced linguistic exchange between themselves and their students.

- Interaction activates the thought processes of another and solidifies one's own thinking.

- Talking with others, either in pairs or small groups, allows for oral rehearsal of learning.

It is important to encourage students to elaborate on their verbal responses and challenge them to go beyond "yes" and "no" answers:

"Tell me more about that."
"What do you mean by . . . ?"
"What else . . . ?"
"How do you know?"

It is also important to allow wait time for students to formulate answers. If necessary, the teacher can also call on another student to extend his or her classmate's response.

All students, including English language learners, benefit from instruction that frequently includes a variety of grouping configurations. It is recommended that at least two different grouping structures be used during a lesson:

- **Flexible small groups**
  o To promote multiple perspectives
  o To encourage collaboration

- **Partnering**
  o To provide practice opportunities
  o To scaffold instruction
  o To give assistance before independent practice

Additionally, teachers should provide activities that allow interaction with varied student groupings.

- Grouping students homogeneously by language proficiency, language background, and/or ability levels facilitates conversation.

- Heterogeneous variety maintains students' interest.

- Movement from whole class, to partners, to small group increases student involvement.

- Heterogeneous grouping can challenge students to a higher level and provide good student models.

- Varying group structures increases the preferred mode of instruction for students.

Cooperative Learning Ideas

Teachers can structure tasks, problems, or activities in ways that encourage students to work together. Here are a few examples.

- **Information gap activities**: Each student in a group has only one or two pieces of the information needed to solve the puzzle or problem. Students must work together, sharing information, while practicing their language and using critical thinking skills.

- **Jigsaw**: A reading task is divided by chunking text into manageable parts (one or two pages); students pool their information.

- **Roundtable:** Small groups of students sit at tables, with one sheet of paper and a pencil. A question, concept, or problem is given to each group by the teacher including open-ended questions and grammar practice; students pass the paper around the table, each writing his or her own response. The teacher circulates throughout the room.

- **Three-step interview:** Students are paired. Each student listens to the other as they respond to a topic question. At the end of three minutes, each pair joins another pair of students and shares what their partners said. This activity provides students with a good way to practice language.

- **Writing headlines:** This activity provides a way to practice summarizing an activity, story, or project. The teacher provides models of newspaper or magazine headlines. Students work in pairs writing a headline for an activity. Pairs share their headlines with the rest of the class and the class votes on the most effective headlines.

SKILL 4.5   Apply knowledge of effective strategies for helping ESL students transfer language skills from L1 to L2

It is important to remember that phonological awareness skills developed in one language can transfer to another language. For ELLs, phonological awareness in L1 predicts successful literacy acquisition in both L1 and L2 (see Skill 1.3).

Children learn to read only once. If they are able to read in their native language, they are able to read in English. It is important for ELLs to increase their vocabulary and knowledge of the structure of English, their second language. By building on what the

ELL already knows with regard to literacy, language, and experiences in his or her native language, teachers will be able to improve the reading level of the ELL in English. For this reason, it is necessary to evaluate the ELL in his or her first, native, or heritage language in order to initiate the best reading instruction in English.

Teachers can also use the similarities and differences of the different languages to teach learning strategies. For example, the adjective comes before the noun in English but in Spanish it comes after the noun. A text written in English is expected to have a main idea and several supporting details to explain or support it. Other languages are more descriptive and depend on the symbolism or beauty of the language to convey the writer's meaning. By using the concept of cognates, both true and false, teachers can improve vocabulary development.

Schumm (2006) emphasizes that not only the reading-level characteristics, but also the differences between L1 and L2, are important because these may influence the assumed level of the student. Some of the questions she proposes to elicit these similarities and differences provide further evaluation of reading-level characteristics:

- Is the L1 writing system logographic like Arabic, syllabic like Cherokee, or alphabetic like English and Greek?

- How does the L1 syntax compare with the L2 syntax?

- Are the spelling patterns phonetic with consistent grapheme-phoneme relationships (e.g., Spanish or French) or are there multiple vowel sounds (e.g., English)?

- Do students read from left to right and top to bottom in their L1?

- Are there true cognates (Spanish, *instrucción* and English, *instruction*) and false cognates (Spanish, *librería* [bookstore] and English, *library*) that will help or confuse the ELL?

- Are the discourse patterns and writing styles of L1 and L2 similar or different?

- Are questions with known answers asked or are rhetorical questions asked?

- Is L1 writing style circular, with long sentences and many details (e.g., Spanish) or linear, with the minimum number of facts or supporting details needed to support the main idea (e.g., English)?

SKILL 4.6   **Apply knowledge of individual differences (e.g., developmental characteristics, cultural and language background, academic strengths, learning styles) to select instructional strategies and resources that facilitate communicative language development**

It is important to develop instruction based on the ELL's individual needs. A number of activities can be used to facilitate the ELL in communicative language.

Pairs and group activities in which students can participate and feel valued are important. In such groupings, students of different cultural and academic backgrounds work together and participate actively. In addition, teachers can at times pair individuals with different strengths, so that students can learn from each other. Grouping increases the comfort level of the students, especially quiet students and those who are struggling with English. Cooperative grouping also gives opportunities for students to share ideas and information, which promotes problem solving.

Student-centered learning instruction has the benefit of catering to students' individual needs, increasing student opportunities to perform, and increasing each student's personal sense of relevance and achievement. Furthermore, it leads to fewer teacher-dominated activities, so that students individually, in pairs, or in small groups work on different tasks and projects that cater to their different ability levels and learning styles.

See Skill 3.2 for a fuller discussion.

SKILL 4.7   **Know how to provide appropriate feedback in response to students' developing English language skills**

Ur (1996) defines feedback as "information given to the learner about his or her performance of a learning task, usually with the objective of improving this performance." This feedback can be as simple as a thumbs-up, a grade on a quiz or test, a raised eyebrow when the student makes a mistake, or comments in the margin of an essay.

Feedback has two main aspects: assessment and correction. Typically, a grade assigned on a written paper, replying to an oral response, simply calling on another student, or a comment such as "Fair" at the end of a written paragraph are used in the language classroom as ways of assessing performance. In correction, comments on a specific aspect of the ELL's performance are given: better or additional alternatives may be suggested, an explanation of why the ELL's answer is incorrect or partially correct may be given, or the teacher may elicit a better response from the student.

Research suggests that not all errors need correcting. Different theories look at mistakes in different ways:

- **Audio-lingualism:** Learners should make few mistakes because they learn in small, controlled steps, so corrections are meaningless.

- **Interlanguage:** Mistakes are an important factor in language learning; by correcting them the learner's interlanguage approaches the target language (Selinker, 1972, 1992).

- **Communicative approach**: Not all mistakes need to be corrected. Correct only those mistakes that interfere with meaning.

- **Monitor theory:** Correction does not lead to language acquisition. Learners need comprehensible input so that they can acquire the target language (Krashen, 1982).

COMPETENCY 5

THE ESL TEACHER UNDERSTANDS HOW TO PROMOTE STUDENTS' LITERACY DEVELOPMENT IN ENGLISH

SKILL 5.1   **Know applicable Texas Essential Knowledge and Skills (TEKS), especially the English language arts and reading curriculum as it relates to ESL, and know how to design and implement appropriate instruction to address TEKS related to the reading and writing strands**

The following website details the Texas English language arts curriculum: http://ritter.tea.state.tx.us/rules/tac/chapter110/.

The International Reading Association (1997) issued a position statement on the place of phonics in reading instruction. This position paper asserts that phonics has an important place in beginning reading instruction, primary teachers value and teach phonics, and effective phonics is integrated into the total language arts program. To help children learn phonics, teaching analytical phonics in context seems to work better than teaching synthetic phonics in isolation (e.g., on worksheets).

Reading Development

Some of the techniques for beginning reading development, skills, and strategies are as follows:

- Teaching children to understand sentences, texts, and other materials is better than trying to teach the word skills in isolation.

- Children can learn the alphabet principles by alphabetizing lists of spelling words or groups of objects.

- Simple techniques such as holding up the left hand and recognizing the letter "L" can help children remember which side of the text to begin reading first.

- Learning to decode words is best achieved by practicing while reading.

- Sight words can be memorized.

- Three major types of context clues are syntactic (word order, word endings, function of words in a sentence), semantic (meaning clues), and phonemes and graphemes (/ph/ may sound like /f/ as in photograph, /ch/ sometimes sounds like /k/ as in chemistry).

- Reading fluency may be improved by observing the following strategies (among others): reread for clarity and to improve understanding, ask for help when confused, realize that "There is no such thing as a stupid question." Venn diagrams, webs, and other graphics may be helpful in organizing texts for easier understanding.

- Vocabulary cards or dictionaries may help ELLs to recall words they don't know. Word walls and instruction on idioms, antonyms, synonyms, and homonyms are useful.

- Learning the structure of sentence patterns, question forms, and their punctuation can help the ELL to determine meaning.

Vocabulary Development

Research has shown that the same 1,000 words (approximately) make up 84 percent of the words used in conversation and 74 percent of the words in academic texts (*The Nation*, 2001). The second most frequently used 1,000 words increases the percentages to 90 percent of the words used in conversation and 78 percent used in academic texts. The ELL needs to understand 95 percent to achieve comprehension of the academic text. ELLs need to acquire the 2,000 most used words and work on academic content words at the same time. In order to help students acquire the vocabulary they need for school, consider the following:

- Vocabulary development for young children is increased using the same methods used with native speaker beginning readers: ample exposure to print, word walls, realia, signs on objects around the room, and so on.

- Older children may take advantage of all these methods in addition to studying true and false cognates, creating personal dictionaries, journal writing between themselves and their teacher, and using learning strategies to augment their vocabulary.

- Other strategies, from Peregoy and Boyle (2008), are as follows:
  o Activate the prior knowledge of the ELL.
  o Repeat the new word in meaningful contexts.
  o Explore the word in depth through demonstrations, direct experience, concrete examples, and applications to real life.
  o Have students explain concepts and ideas in writing and speaking using the new words.
  o Provide explicit strategy instruction so that students can independently understand and use the new words.

Writing Development

The writing process needs to be taught, since many students come from backgrounds in which writing a text or paper is very different from U.S. conventions. They may be unfamiliar with the concept of planning the paper, doing research, organizing the material, developing a thesis statement, deciding on methods of development, drafting, revising, and editing. Rubrics can be devised that are appropriate to process writing and take into consideration both the process and the product.

There are many ways to get students to practice writing without grading the writing: learning logs, journals, and quick-writes. Teachers can devise prompts that allow ELLs to reflect on their learning and class discussions or explore new ideas. They may rewrite complex ideas in their own words and compare, evaluate, critique, or interpret. At the end of the period, students may quickly write what they learned during the class. ELLs can write dialogue, either in pairs or individually. They can try using vocabulary words from their text in comprehensible paragraphs. Another idea is to write from the perspective of another person, place, or thing. (Adapted from Zwiers, 2008)

On the other hand, these students may be fairly sophisticated in their manipulation of language. However, their language may value other aspects of writing that are very different from the American English idea of a sentence (subject-verb-object) or a paragraph (the topic sentence and its supporting details). In essays, the idea of developing sentences of varying lengths and structures, and connecting them through the skillful use of connectors, will have to be taught through modeling and examples. Supplying ample resources, such as dictionaries and lists of vocabulary conventions or connectors, will be invaluable to ELLs in upper levels.

Also, students who are learning to write need to read as much as possible of the genre that they are going to be writing about. As writing takes place in multiple genres (narrative prose, poetry, mathematical proofs, historical accounts, case studies, essays, emails, and letters), students should be exposed to each particular type of writing—its organization, the thinking behind the form, the grammar, and the correct terms used in each genre—so that they are able to replicate the appropriate phrases and syntax in their writing. As students outside the mainstream will not have had as much exposure to the models as native speakers, it is necessary to point out the conventions of each genre as it is studied in the classroom.

Skill 5.2 Understand the interrelatedness of listening, speaking, reading, and writing and use this knowledge to select and use effective strategies for developing students' literacy in English

Fluency is developed over time through extensive practice in both speaking and reading. Ample opportunities should be given to ELLs to develop their speaking and listening abilities to help them achieve more oral fluency.

Increasing Oral Fluency

Role plays, skits, poems, singing, and telephone dialogues are good ways to increase oral fluency. Fluency in reading interacts with oral fluency. Wide exposure to print and reading will increase both reading and oral fluency. The two are intertwined.

Fluent readers are able to grasp chunks of language, read for meaning (and not word by word), and decode automatically. They are confident readers who are able to self-monitor, and to maintain comprehension. Specific instruction devoted to these areas should improve fluency rates in slower readers.

Developing Literacy in English

Literacy is a complex set of skills that comprise the interrelated processes of reading and writing. Reading requires decoding, accurate and fluent word recognition, and comprehension at the word, phrase, sentence, and text levels. Writing requires automatic letter formation and/or keyboarding, accurate and fluent spelling, sentence construction, and the ability to compose a variety of different text structures with coherence and cohesion.

Literacy involves the integration of speaking, listening, and critical thinking. Young children use their oral language skills to learn to read, whereas older children use their reading ability to further their language learning. The instructional components necessary for reading and writing include phonemic awareness, phonics, vocabulary building, fluency development, comprehension, text structure, and writing process strategies, as well as prerequisite writing skills such as handwriting, spelling, and grammar.

A survey of research points to the following indicators of effective instructional literacy practices:

- Motivating students according to their unique needs and interests

- Providing direct explicit instruction of reading and writing skills and strategies based on ongoing student assessment

- Modeling the effective thinking skills that good readers and writers employ

- Devoting 50 percent of the students' instructional time on a daily basis to reading and writing in the classroom

- Activating students' prior knowledge to help them make connections between what they know and what they would like to learn

- Providing opportunities for students to make text and writing connections to their lives, forms of media, and the world

- Offering both guided and independent reading experiences

- Differentiating instruction with a plentiful supply of multilevel books to accommodate interests and ability levels

- Motivating readers by offering a choice of books to read that are at their independent reading level, that they can read with accuracy, fluency, and comprehension

- Promoting conversation through purposeful and guided discussion about a book, piece of writing, or topic

- Guiding discussions through open-ended questioning

- Creating a more personable learning environment

- Designing projects that excite and engage students as opposed to engaging in short disconnected tasks (integration of subjects)

- Assessing student work based on common rubrics

SKILL 5.3 **Understand that English is an alphabetic language and apply effective strategies for developing ESL students' phonological knowledge and skills (e.g., phonemic awareness skills, knowledge of English letter-sound associations, knowledge of common English phonograms) and sight-word vocabularies (e.g., phonetically irregular words, high-frequency words)**

Fluency is based on a foundation of oral language skills, phonemic awareness, familiarity with letter forms, and efficient decoding skills. A combination of instruction in decoding and reading comprehension is required for students to achieve high levels of reading skill.

Teaching decoding skills is considered to be one of the effective methods of reading instruction. The emphasis is on teaching the phoneme-grapheme correspondences. In order to develop effective reading skills, students should aim for **automaticity**; in other words, the brain process of decoding letter sounds becomes automatic. Automaticity leads to fluent reading, whereby the brain may process many letters, sounds, and words at the same time, which is positively related to students' achievement in reading.

Once decoding skills are mastered, more attention can be given to mastering the overall meaning of a phrase or sentence (comprehension). However, students still need explicit instruction in developing strategies to improve their comprehension skills.

Phonics and other linguistic approaches to teaching reading are important in terms of word identification skills. Accurate and rapid word recognition leads to fluency in reading. When the reader's decoding skills become automatic, he or she is able to focus attention on constructing meaning.

For readers who have not yet reached automaticity of decoding skills, reading is a slow, laborious struggle. Fluent readers are more likely than struggling readers to engage in extensive reading. In the case of ESL learners, however, reading more will not achieve fluency. Expert teacher guidance is necessary for ELLs to reach reading fluency.

Several studies have focused on the types of instruction that would increase fluency in readers. These instructional practices include:

- Modeled reading
- Repeated reading of familiar text
- Wide independent reading
- Coached reading of appropriately selected materials
- Chunking of text
- Word reading practice

SKILL 5.4   **Know factors that affect ESL students' reading comprehension (e.g., vocabulary, text structures, cultural references) and apply effective strategies for facilitating ESL students' reading comprehension in English**

During efficient reading, incoming textual data is processed (bottom-up), which activates appropriate higher-level schemas (top-down) against which the reader tries to give the text a coherent interpretation. The reader makes predictions on the basis of these top-down processes and then searches the text for confirmation or rejection of these partially satisfied higher-order schemas.

Reading Comprehension

Many people wait for a reading passage to present the information in an organized way for them. However, reading comprehension is a highly complex area where successful readers use reading strategies in each of the three distinct phases of reading—prereading, reading, and postreading—to successfully understand a text (Peregoy & Boyle, 2008).

- The purposes of the **prereading phase** are for teachers to build background knowledge through anticipation guides or field trips, motivate the reader with structured overviews or films, and establish the purpose using experiments or pictures.

- The purposes of the **reading phase** are to read, based upon the established purpose, using learning logs or annotating texts to record information; improve comprehension by directed reading-thinking activities and asking questions; and utilize background knowledge by studying headings and subheadings and answering questions.

- The purposes of the **postreading phase** are to help the student with organizing and remembering information through activities such as artwork, maps, or summaries and use the information in reporting, making a film, or publishing.

Some of the techniques students need to be able to master in reading comprehension include the following:

- Skimming to extract main idea
- Scanning for specific information
- Predicting based on prior knowledge
- Restating the information to indicate comprehension of the text
- Recognizing inferred information
- Sounding out unfamiliar words, guessing at their meaning based on previous understanding of the text
- Summarizing the text

Teachers can guide students through these steps by using scaffolding techniques and giving support as needed.

Reading Comprehension for ELLs

Children's and young adult literature includes parables, fables, fairy tales, folktales, myths, legends, novels, romances, poetry, drama, and novels. ELLs need to be taught the intricacies of plot, point of view, setting, characterization, and other literary terms just as their native speaking classmates do. Many of these terms are universal, but the instructor should be aware that the literature of another culture may vary considerably from its English counterpart. Encouraging and promoting a significant amount of reading of the different genres both inside and outside the classroom is one way to introduce these elements to students.

Reading classes should include instruction of the grammatical elements that typically occur over large stretches of text. Authentic texts contain more complex grammatical constructions, like anaphoric reference and cohesive devices, which result in second-language readers having difficulty synthesizing information across sentences and paragraphs.

Vocabulary building is an important aspect of reading instruction in order to avoid breakdown in the process of reading. The teacher can help students read a passage by preparing them with a brief list of some of the most important terms, together with their meanings in the context before they read. The teacher should select for preteaching only those words that help to read the text accurately and critically.

The cultural dimension to reading involves one's purposes for reading and the attitude one holds toward the book and its content. Therefore, the teacher needs to utilize techniques and instructional practices that take into account attitudes based on the cultural background of learners. One effective technique is to give students ample opportunities to work in pairs and small groups in which they share with each other the process of reading and literacy in their own cultures.

SKILL 5.5 Apply knowledge of effective strategies for helping students transfer literacy knowledge and skills from L1 to L2

Peregoy and Boyle (2008) state that literacy scaffolding helps ELLs with reading and writing at a level that would otherwise be impossible for them. Scaffolding allows ELLs to work at their level in both reading and writing, and at the same time challenges them to reach their next level of development. To help students achieve their level, several criteria are suggested:

- Use of functional, meaningful communication found in whole texts
- Use of language and discourse patterns that repeat themselves and are predictable
- A model (from teacher or peers) for understanding and producing particular written language patterns
- Support of students at their instructional level, which Krashen refers to as $i + 1$
- Discarding supports when the student no longer needs them

Instruction in the First Language

Keeping in mind the scaffolding theory, teachers may use the first language in instruction—if they know it. This is not always possible. In many states, hundreds of language communities are represented in the statewide school system. A danger of this method is that some students become dependent on instruction in their first language and are reluctant to utilize their knowledge of the second language.

However, for most children, instruction in their first language has numerous advantages. First, language instruction lowers the affective filter by reducing tension, anxiety, and even fear, thus permitting faster learning; it can clarify misunderstandings in the second language content; and it can be used to explain how the two languages differ or are the same with respect to different types of reading texts or writing tasks.

Activating Prior Knowledge

Schemas need to be activated to draw upon the previous knowledge and learning of the ELL, especially when the ELL may not have had experiences similar to those of learners in mainstream culture. The use of graphics to encourage prereading thought about a topic (e.g., brainstorming, web maps, and organizational charts) activates this knowledge and shows how information is organized in students' minds. Schumm (2006) states that research has shown:

- More prior knowledge permits a reader to understand and remember more (Brown, Bransford, Ferrara & Campione, 1983).

- Prior knowledge must be activated to improve comprehension (Bransford & Johnson, 1972).

- Failure to activate prior knowledge is one cause of poor readers (Paris & Lindauer, 1976).

- Good readers accept new information if they are convinced by an author's arguments. Likewise, they may reject ideas when they conflict with a reader's prior knowledge (Pressley, 2000).

SKILL 5.6   **Apply knowledge of individual differences (e.g., developmental characteristics, cultural and language background, academic strengths, learning styles) to select instructional strategies and resources that facilitate ESL students' literacy development**

The ELLs who have arrived in the school system in upper elementary or secondary grades may have limited literacy skills or age-appropriate academic content knowledge in their native language. Academic language may be new and different from their previous experiences. They may have been forced to develop survival skills. Some may be from rural areas where they learned about life cycles, reproduction, and weather. City dwellers may have been involved in the buying, selling, and bartering of goods. Even though the ELL may not know how to read or write, many cultures have strong traditions of oral literature handed down from generation to generation.

One way to bridge these gaps and difficulties is by using the Cognitive Academic Language Learning Approach (CALLA; see Skill 8.4). The CALLA teacher needs to first introduce basic literacy skills. If possible, these should be introduced in the native or heritage language of the child.

For older students, the Language Experience Approach (LEA; see Skill 6.2) has proven effective. Another technique to use with older students is to have them read such everyday items as signs, ads, and menus. There is an immediate association between these practical materials and the need to learn to read (Chamot & O'Malley, 1994).

- Creating **illustrated autobiographies** ("All about Me" or "The Story of My Life") can help ease ELLs into the academic challenges of a new school and culture. Students use as much English as they can and draw pictures to illustrate other points. This is an integrative activity because ELLs are not singled out but are part of the group.

- **Dialogue journals** can be used with students of all ages. Provide all students with blank journals and allow them to draw or write in the language of their choice. The instructor should respond to the journals periodically. Journals are an excellent way to develop a personal relationship with students while at the same time introducing literacy to the class.

- **Themes** such as "Where We Were Born" or "Family Origins" make good starting points to learn about home cultures and activate prior knowledge of all students.

(Adapted from Peregoy & Boyle, 2008)

SKILL 5.7   **Know personal factors that affect ESL students' English literacy development (e.g., interrupted schooling, literacy status in the primary language, prior literacy experiences) and apply effective strategies for addressing these factors**

Literacy development is affected not only by the students' educational background but also by the educational background of their families. With respect to individual students, it is paramount to note that some adolescent ELLs need to learn to read for the first time, whereas others are building second- or third-language literacy with already developed first language literacy (Peregoy & Boyle, 2008). Those students who lack literacy skills in their first language have inadequate skills to succeed in school and need basic as well as advanced literacy development.

Factors Affecting an ELL's Literacy Development

Literacy requires a number of cognitive and metacognitive skills that ELLs can transfer from their first language to their second or third language. In addition, students literate in their first language have more prior knowledge to help them comprehend the content of the text.

The educational background of the ELLs gives them the advantage of transferring their first-language literacy skills to their second language and using their prior literacy knowledge to understand the new information. With respect to writing, research has shown that students who lacked first-language literacy strategies displayed a similar lack of strategies for writing in their second language. Mohan and Lo (1985) suggest that students who have not developed good strategies in their first language will not have developed strategies to transfer to their second language. Similarly, transfer of knowledge from L1 literacy helps students brainstorm information to write about the topic at hand.

Family literacy of the English language learners also has an impact on their literacy development. The educational level of parents has a great influence on literacy development, reflecting the family's attitude toward education and the value they give to success in school. Parents with positive attitudes toward education are more involved in school activities and keep track of their child's progress. They attend parent-teacher conferences and are a part of the learning process.

Parents who read books to children from an early age—and have books, newspapers, magazines, and other reading materials available at home—facilitate their children's literacy development. These families spend time reading together and encourage critical thinking and higher-order skills in their children. These positive attributes help students develop skills that are critical for success in school.

Drawing upon the ELLs' Literacy Experiences

Research suggests that, contrary to many popular myths, immigrant families, poor families, and other minority group families do value literacy and education. Although literacy varies in different families, it serves many functions in families living below the poverty level, families in which English is not the primary language, and families with low educational levels (Peregoy & Boyle, 2008). Teachers need to be perceptive and draw upon the child's home language and literacy experiences so that the child is better served by beginning literacy instruction.

Encouraging home involvement in the literacy process is critical. Family members model reading and writing every time they read the newspaper or magazine, make a shopping list, note an appointment on a calendar, discuss their work schedule, or question the newest charges on the phone bill. Many children come from societies in which oral storytelling traditions (e.g., Navajo, Spanish, Hmong, or African American) provide excellent foundations for literacy development.

Nevertheless, little research has been conducted about how to teach ELLs with limited literacy in their first language—whether a young child or an older one. If feasible, students should first learn to read in their native language and later in the second language. When instruction is begun in English, many ESOL practitioners believe that the same methods used to teach the native speaker will be beneficial to the ELL because similar literacy patterns will probably emerge. Older learners may be able to progress more rapidly because they use their worldly experiences to help them with comprehension and communication.

National reading authorities recommend phonemic awareness, phonics, reading fluency, and comprehension as the keys to success in achieving literacy. All of these elements should be considered in meaningful contexts rather than in isolation. Instruction in specific strategies (e.g., summarizing, retelling, and answering questions) will help ELLs to become independent readers and writers.

COMPETENCY 6

THE ESL TEACHER UNDERSTANDS HOW TO PROMOTE STUDENTS' CONTENT-AREA LEARNING, ACADEMIC LANGUAGE DEVELOPMENT, AND ACHIEVEMENT ACROSS THE CURRICULUM

SKILL 6.1   **Apply knowledge of effective practices, resources, and materials for providing content-based ESL instruction, engaging students in critical thinking, and developing students' cognitive academic language proficiency**

It is important to implement powerful instructional strategies that actively engage students from linguistically and culturally diverse backgrounds instead of allowing them to be passive participants or observers. Chamot and O'Malley (1994) stated that teachers need to be aware of their students' approaches to learning and know how to expand the students' repertoire of learning strategies.

Language-Sensitive Content Instruction

According to Arreaga-Mayer (1998), language-sensitive content instruction based on effective and efficient learning strategies must: (a) be effective for culturally and linguistically homogenous learning groups; (b) lead to high levels of student and student-to-student active engagement in learning; (c) foster higher-order cognitive processes; (d) enable students to encourage extended discourse in English; (e) be feasible to implement on a small-group or class-wide basis; (f) be socially acceptable to teachers, students, and parents; and (g) be responsive to cultural and personal diversity.

Arreaga-Mayer puts forward constructs for effective instruction to linguistically and culturally diverse students:

1. Challenge
   - Implicit (cognitive challenge, use of higher-order questions)
   - Explicit (high but reasonable expectations)

2. Involvement
   - Active involvement of all students

3. Success
   - Reasonable activities that students can complete successfully

4. Scaffolding/cognitive strategies
   - Visual organizers, adequate background information, and support provided by teachers to students by thinking aloud, building on and clarifying their input

5. Mediation/feedback
   - Strategies provided to students
   - Frequency and comprehensibility stressed

6. Collaborative/cooperative learning

7. Techniques for second-language acquisition/sheltered English
   - Extended discourse
   - Consistent language
   - Incorporation of students' language

8. Respect for cultural diversity
   - Respect and knowledge of cultural diversity

Peer-Mediated Instruction

Peer-mediated instruction is effective in promoting higher levels of language and academic learning and social interaction. Research has shown that cooperative, peer-mediated instruction contributes more to content mastery than do whole-class instruction, workbook activities, and question-answer sessions. This method gives ELLs opportunities to actively practice a concept, the amount of discourse produced, the degree of negotiation of meaning, and the amount of comprehensible linguistic input.

The essential components of peer-mediated learning strategies are
   - Cooperative incentives
   - Group rewards
   - Individual accountability
   - Task structures

Students with varied academic abilities and language proficiency levels work together in pairs and small groups toward a common goal. In these groups, the success of one student depends on the help of the others. The learning task assigned to groups varies, but the format of learning always includes interaction and interdependence among the students.

Peer Tutoring

Peer tutoring is a method developed to improve the acquisition and retention of basic academic skills. In this method, students are either paired randomly or matched by ability or language proficiency each week. Students' roles are switched during the daily tutoring session, allowing each child to be both the tutor/teacher and the tutee/student. Students are trained in the procedures necessary to act as tutors and tutees. The following are four basic components of this method:

1. Weekly competing teams (culturally, linguistically, and ability heterogeneous grouping)

2. Highly structured teaching procedure (content material, teams, pairing, error correction, system of rewards)

3. Daily, contingent, individual tutee point earning and public postings of individual and team scores

4. Direct practice of functional academic and language skills to master

Teaching Academic English

Academic tasks tend to increase in their cognitive demands as students progress in their schooling but the context becomes increasingly reduced. ELLs who have not developed Cognitive Academic Language Proficiency (CALP) need additional teacher support to achieve success. Contextual support in the form of realia, demonstrations, pictures, graphs, and so on provide the ELL with scaffolding and reduce the language difficulty level of the task. Both content and ESOL teachers should incorporate teaching academic skills in their lessons.

The following are essential elements to include in teaching academic English:

1. Integrate listening, speaking, reading, and writing skills in all lessons for all proficiencies.

2. Teach the components and processes of reading and writing.

3. Focus on vocabulary development.

4. Build and activate prior knowledge.

5. Teach language through content and themes.

6. Use native language strategically.

7. Pair technology with instruction.

8. Motivate ELLs with choice.

SKILL 6.2   **Know instructional delivery practices that are effective in facilitating ESL students' comprehension in content-area classes (e.g., preteaching key vocabulary; helping students apply familiar concepts from their cultural backgrounds and prior experiences to new learning; using hands-on and other experiential learning strategies; using realia, media, and other visual supports to introduce and/or reinforce concepts)**

A number of program models have been developed to meet the needs of language minority students involving the integration of language and content instruction. In one approach, the second or foreign language is used as the medium of instruction for mathematics, science, social studies, and other academic subjects; it is the vehicle used for teaching and acquiring subject-specific knowledge. The focus of the second-language classroom should be on something meaningful, such as academic content. Modification of the target language facilitates language acquisition and makes academic content accessible to second-language learners.

Integrated Approach to Language Teaching

Integrated language and content instruction offers a means by which ESL students can continue their academic or cognitive development while they are also acquiring academic language proficiency. In **theme-based programs**, a language curriculum is developed around selected topics drawn from one content area (e.g., marketing) or from across the curriculum (e.g., pollution and the environment). The theme could be a week or two long and focused on language taught in a meaningful way. The goal is to assist learners in developing general academic language skills through interesting and relevant content. There are a variety of strategies to teach the integrated approach to language teaching, of which the four most important are as follows:

1. **Cooperative learning:** Students of different linguistic and educational backgrounds and different skill levels work together on a common task for a common goal to complete a task pertaining to content being taught in the classroom. The focus is also on an implicit or explicit language feature that students acquire through negotiation of meaning.

2. **Task-based or experiential learning:** Appropriate contexts are provided for developing thinking and study skills as well as language and academic concepts for students at different levels of language proficiency. Students learn by carrying out specific tasks or projects that they complete with a focus on content while also learning language and academic skills.

3. **Whole-language approach:** The philosophy of whole language is based on the concept that students need to experience language as an integrated whole. It focuses on the need for an integrated approach to language instruction within a context that is meaningful to students (Goodman, 1986). The approach is consistent with integrated language and content instruction, as both emphasize

meaningful engagement and authentic language use, and both link oral and written language development (Blanton, 1992). Whole-language strategies that have been implemented in content-centered language classes include dialogue journals, reading response journals, learning logs, process-based writing, and language experience stories (Crandall, 1992).

4. **Graphic organizers:** Graphic organizers are frameworks that provide a "means for organizing and presenting information so that it can be understood, remembered, and applied" (Crandall, 1992). Graphs, realia, tables, maps, flowcharts, timelines, and Venn diagrams are used to help students place information in a comprehensible context. These props enable students to organize information obtained from written or oral texts, develop reading strategies, increase retention, activate schema as a prereading or prelistening activity, and organize ideas during the prewriting stage (Crandall et al., 2002).

Language Experience Approach

An approach that teaches vocabulary and builds prior knowledge about content for readers is the **Language Experience Approach (LEA).** Pressley (2000) states that good readers utilize background knowledge to make inferences that are necessary for understanding a text. This process helps readers create new knowledge from the text (top-down processing). In light of this view, LEA supports children's concept development and vocabulary growth while offering many opportunities for meaningful reading and writing activities. It also helps in the development of shared experiences that expand children's knowledge of the world around them.

In an LEA activity, students create a narrative, which provides the content of the lesson. This approach focuses students' attention on specific experiences in their daily lives such as taking a class walk to collect leaves, blowing bubbles, making popcorn, apple picking, or experimenting with magnets. Students are involved in planning, experiencing, responding to, and recording the experience. The teacher initiates a discussion eliciting narrative from the students while providing appropriate vocabulary. In the end, the students compose oral individual or group stories, which the teacher writes down and reads with students.

SKILL 6.3 **Apply knowledge of individual differences (e.g., developmental characteristics, cultural and language background, academic strengths, learning styles) to select instructional strategies and resources that facilitate ESL students' cognitive-academic language development and content-area learning**

Cognitive processes are used by the learner to organize and direct second-language acquisition. Examples of these processes are problem solving, method of approaching the learning of new information, and choices regarding what to ignore and what to notice (Díaz-Rico & Weed, 2013). Developing these skills leads to language acquisition, but these skills also bridge languages and serve to enhance cognition in the first language.

Research demonstrates that learning and using more than one language

- Enhances problem-solving and analytical skills
- Allows better formation of concepts
- Increases visual-social abilities
- Furthers logical reasoning
- Supports cognitive flexibility

Cognitive skills are any mental skills that are used in the process of acquiring knowledge, including reasoning, perception, and intuition. Using these skills in second-language learning applies L2 vocabulary and sentence patterns to thought processes that have already formed in the L1.

Memorizing the words and rules of a second language is insufficient to integrate the second language into the learner's thought patterns. L2 learners use cognitive processes for **forming rules,** which allow them to understand and create novel utterances. The creation of novel utterances, whether grammatically correct or not, offers proof that the L2 learner is not simply mimicking chunks of prescribed language, but rather is using cognitive processes to acquire the second language. People use their own thinking processes, or cognition, to discover the rules of the language they are acquiring.

Planning what actions to take when confronted with an academic (or social) challenge demonstrates understanding of the problem and the ability to confront it. By engaging cognitive skills, the student can plan where and how to search for information, how to organize it, and how to present the information for review.

Organizational skills may show differences in different cultural contexts. For example, when organizing information for writing, the English speaker starts from a smaller unit and ends at a larger unit. In addresses, for example:

Dr. Randall Price
Department of English as a Second Language
University of Georgia
Athens, GA
USA

A Japanese speaker would begin with the largest unit and end at the smallest one:

USA
Athens, GA
University of Georgia
Department of English as a Second Language
Dr. Randall Price

Teachers cannot assume that their students already have these skills. Even the most basic organizational skill concepts must be glossed or fully taught if necessary.

SKILL 6.4 **Know personal factors that affect ESL students' content-area learning (e.g., prior learning experiences, familiarity with specialized language and vocabulary, familiarity with the structure and uses of textbooks and other print resources) and apply effective strategies for addressing those factors**

The term **affective domain** refers to the feelings and emotions in human behavior that affect how a second language is acquired. Internal and external factors influence the affective domain. ESOL teachers must be aware of each student's personality and must stay especially attuned to the affective factors in their students.

Self-esteem, motivation, anxiety, and attitude all contribute to the second-language acquisition process.

Self-Esteem

Learning a second language puts learners in a vulnerable frame of mind. While some learners are less inhibited about taking risks, all learners can easily be shut down if their comfort level is surpassed. Using teaching techniques that lower stress and emphasize group participation, rather than focusing on individuals getting the right answer, reduces anxiety and encourages learners to attempt to use the new language.

Motivation

Researchers Gardner and Lambert (1972) identified two types of motivation in relation to learning a second language:

- **Instrumental motivation:** acquiring a second language for a specific reason, such as a job

- **Integrative motivation:** acquiring a second language to fulfill a wish to communicate within a different culture

Neither type stands completely alone. Instructors recognize that motivation can be viewed as either a trait or a state. As a trait, motivation is more permanent and culturally acquired. As a state, motivation is considered temporary because it fluctuates depending on rewards and penalties.

Anxiety

Anxiety is inherent in second-language learning. Students are required to take risks, such as speaking in front of their peers. Without a native grasp of the language, second-language learners are unable to express their individuality, which is even more threatening and uncomfortable. However, not all anxiety is debilitative. Bailey's (1983) research on "facilitative anxiety" (anxiety that compels an individual to stay on task) is a positive factor for some learners, closely related to competitiveness.

Attitude

On the one hand, attitude typically evolves from internalized feelings about oneself and one's ability to learn a language. On the other hand, one's attitude about language and the speakers of that language is largely external and is influenced by the surrounding environment of classmates and family.

If nonnative speakers of English experience discrimination because of their accent or cultural status, their attitude toward the value of second-language learning may diminish. Schools can significantly improve the attitude toward L2 learners by encouraging activities between native speakers and ELLs. This endeavor can be particularly beneficial to both groups if students learning the L2 learner's first language work on projects together. When native speakers of English attempt to interact in a second language themselves, they get a chance to appreciate the L2 learner's language skill in their first language, attitudes change, and ELLs have an opportunity to shine as teachers. For many ELLs, these experiences are helpful for maintaining self-esteem during the uncomfortable period of transitioning into a new language and culture.

In some cultures, children who learn a second language at the expense of their primary language might be viewed as "turncoats" by family and friends. This attitude can cause negative feelings about school in general and can adversely affect second-language acquisition. In the Mexican-American community, for instance, "pocho" is a derogatory term used to refer to Mexicans who speak English and have given up their first culture. Many factors limit successful assimilation, including age, ethnicity, religious and political affiliations, and economic level (Thompson, 1996).

Native American leaders are often resistant to English acquisition because it frequently signals a loss of the native first language. In 2000, Arizona voters ended bilingual education in their state by a 63 percent majority. Twenty-one of 26 states have passed official English laws since 1981. Some view this movement as a "war on diversity" (Reyner, 1997). Those who are anxious to succeed in the English-speaking world may face disapproval from significant members of their families and communities.

Fewer than half of Native American languages still are spoken, and many of those are used by only a handful of people. Evangeline Parsons Yazzie, a professor at Northern Arizona University, says, "Television is robbing our children of language. Older people who speak only Navajo are alone." Navajo Nation president, Kelsey Begaye: "The Navajo way of life is based on our language. The stories, traditions, and customs of our people cannot be fully transmitted, understood, or communicated in non-Navajo languages" (Reyhner, 1997). Navajo children may feel they are betraying their culture as they attempt to assimilate by using English.

COMPETENCY 7

THE ESL TEACHER UNDERSTANDS FORMAL AND INFORMAL ASSESSMENT PROCEDURES
AND INSTRUMENTS USED IN ESL PROGRAMS AND USES ASSESSMENT RESULTS TO PLAN
AND ADAPT INSTRUCTION

SKILL 7.1   **Know basic concepts, issues, and practices related to test design, development, and interpretation, and use this knowledge to select, adapt, and develop assessments for different purposes in the ESL program (e.g., diagnosis, program evaluation, proficiency)**

In order to understand assessment procedures, it is necessary to be able to distinguish between different tests used in assessment.

Types of Tests

Many different types of tests are used for various purposes. Hughes (1989) makes a number of distinctions between test types, which are as follows:

- **Proficiency tests:** Proficiency tests are designed to measure student proficiency in the target language irrespective of any prior training in that language. Criteria are based on what candidates have to be able to do in the language in order to be considered proficient for a particular purpose (e.g., for college/university or employment as a United Nations translator).

- **Achievement tests:** Unlike proficiency tests, achievement tests are directly related to language courses and establish how successful the students or the course itself are in achieving the objectives.

- **Diagnostic tests:** Diagnostic tests are used to identify students' strengths and weaknesses. The aim is to determine what further needs to be taught to the students and which students can benefit from individual instruction.

- **Placement tests:** Placement tests are typically used to determine the level of class in which the student should be placed according to his or her abilities.

- **Direct vs. indirect testing:** "Direct" and "indirect" refer to approaches to test construction. Direct testing requires candidates to perform precisely the skill that is to be measured. For example, if we want to know how well candidates can write compositions, the test would ask them to write compositions. Indirect testing tries to determine the abilities that underlie the skills which are important for the testing purpose. An example would be a paper-and-pencil test for testing pronunciation ability, in which candidates have to identify pairs of words that rhyme.

- **Discrete-point vs. integrative testing:** Discrete-point testing refers to the testing of one element at a time, item by item. It might contain a number of items, each testing a particular grammatical structure. Integrative testing makes use of a combination of language elements for a candidate to complete a task. These could range from taking notes while listening to a lecture to writing a composition.

- **Norm-referenced vs. criterion-referenced testing:** Norm-referenced tests relate one candidate's performance to that of other candidates. A norm-referenced test does not tell directly what the student is capable of doing in the language. The test score could place the student in the top 10 percent of candidates who have taken the test, or show that a candidate did better than 60 percent of those who took it. A criterion-referenced test classifies people according to whether or not they are able to perform some task or set of tasks successfully. The candidates who perform these tasks pass the test, irrespective of how the rest of the candidates scored on the test.

- **Objective vs. subjective testing:** The difference between objective and subjective testing is in the methods of scoring. If no judgment is required by the scorer during the scoring process, the test is objective (e.g., multiple choice tests). However, if some judgment by the scorer is required, the test is subjective.

- **Communicative language testing:** A lot of discussions have emphasized the importance of measuring students' ability to take part in acts of communication (including reading and listening) and the best way to do this kind of measurement. A number of informal testing methods can be used to achieve this purpose: for example, teacher observation of students working on a task in groups, or students' comprehension of a reading passage that enables them to successfully complete a task.

Quality in ELL Assessment Testing

The constructs of reliability and validity are crucial in assessing ELLs because of the high stakes involved in testing in today's schools. Decisions about schools, teachers, and students are based on these tests. A viable assessment test for ELLs will have the following three attributes: validity, reliability, and practicality.

Validity

An assessment test can be considered **valid** only if it measures what it asserts to measure. If an ELL assessment test claims to measure oral proficiency, the test should include a section in which instructors ask the ELL to pronounce certain words, listen to the instructor's pronunciation to determine if it is correct, and ask the learner to respond directly to the instructor's questions.

According to Díaz-Rico and Weed (1995/2013), "Empirical validity is a measure of how effectively a test relates to some other known measure." There are different types of validity: **predictive** and **concurrent**. Predictive empirical validity is concerned with the possible outcomes of test performance; concurrent empirical validity is connected with another variable for measurement. For example, if a learner shows high English speech proficiency in class, the instructor would have the expectation that the learner would perform well during an oral proficiency exam.

Reliability

An assessment test can be considered **reliable** only if similar scores result when the test is taken a second time. Factors such as anxiety, hunger, tiredness, and uncomfortable environmental conditions should not cause a huge fluctuation in the learner's score. Typically, if a learner earns a score of 90% on a test that was created by the instructor, then averages predict that the learner probably scored 45% on one half of the test and 45% on the other half, regardless of the structure of the test items.

Practicality

A test that proves both valid and reliable might be cost- or time-prohibitive. The ideal assessment test would be one that is easy to administer and easy to grade, and that includes testing items similar to what the learners have experienced in class. However, when learners encounter test items such as writing journals, then practicality becomes an issue. A writing journal, although an excellent method for learners to explore their critical literacy skills and track language achievement progress, can be difficult to grade due to its subjective content, and it may not act as a fair representation of what learners have encountered in class.

SKILL 7.2   **Apply knowledge of formal and informal assessments used in the ESL classroom and know their characteristics, uses, and limitations**

There are a multitude of tests for evaluating, assessing, and placing ELLs in appropriate programs. Each test can test a narrow range of language skills (such as discrete-point tests designed to measure grammar sub-skills or vocabulary).

A language test should be chosen on the basis of the information it gives, the appropriateness of the instrument for the purpose, and the soundness of the test content.

Language has more than two hundred dimensions that can be evaluated, and yet most tests assess fewer than twelve of them. Therefore, all language testing should be performed cautiously; backed up by teacher observations, oral interviews, and family life variables; and grounded in school records.

Formal Assessments for ELLs

Language Placement Tests

A language placement test is designed to determine whether a student should be placed within a specific program. The school district may design its own instrument or use a standardized test.

Language Proficiency Tests

Language proficiency tests measure how well students have met certain standards in a particular language. The standards have been predetermined and are unrelated to any course of study, curriculum, or program. These tests are frequently used to determine whether to enter or exit a student to or from a particular program. Examples of language proficiency tests are

- AAPPL: ACTFL Assessment of Performance toward Proficiency in Languages
- TELPAS: Texas English Language Proficiency Assessment System
- TOEFL: Test of English as a Foreign Language (collegiate level)

Language Achievement Tests

Language achievement tests relate directly to a specific curriculum or course of study. The tests include language sub-skills, reading comprehension, parts of speech, and other mechanical parts of the language such as spelling, punctuation, and paragraphing. Examples include unit, midterm, and final exams.

Diagnostic Language Tests

Diagnostic language tests are designed to identify individual students' strengths and weaknesses in languages. They are generally administered by speech therapists or psychologists in clinical settings when specific language learning problems are present.

Informal Assessments for ELLs

The following are examples of alternative assessments that offer options for an instructor (informal assessment).

Portfolios

A portfolio is a collection of the student's work over a period of time (report cards, creative writing, drawing, and so on) that also functions as an assessment, because it

- Indicates a range of competencies and skills
- Is representative of instructional goals and academic growth

Conferencing

When used as an assessment tool, an individual conference allows the instructor to evaluate a student's progress or regression. In conferences, students also learn techniques for self-evaluation.

Oral Interviews

Teachers can use oral interviews to evaluate the language a student is using or the student's ability to provide content information when asked questions. Both of these purposes are instrumental for further instructional planning.

Teacher Observation

When observation is used as an assessment tool, the instructor observes student behavior during an activity alone or within a group. Before the observation occurs, the instructor may create a numerical scale to rate desired outcomes.

Documentation

Documenting the student's activity shares similarities with teacher observations. However, documentation tends to transpire over a period of time whereas observations are isolated events.

Interviews

As an assessment tool, informal interviewing allows instructors to evaluate the student's level of English proficiency. The interview also helps the instructor to identify potential problem areas which may require correctional strategies.

Self-Assessment

Students benefit tremendously from a self-assessment, because through the process of self-analysis they begin to think for themselves. Instructors need to provide guidance as well as the criteria for success.

Student Journals

Student journals have many record-keeping uses that can contribute toward an assessment. Students also benefit from journals because they are useful for promoting an inner dialogue.

Story or Text Retelling

Retelling a story is a useful assessment form. Students respond orally and can be assessed on how well they describe events in the story or text, their response to the story, and their language proficiency.

Experiments and Demonstrations

Students complete an experiment or demonstration and present it through an oral or written report. Students can be evaluated on their understanding of the concept, explanation of the scientific method, and their language proficiency.

SKILL 7.3   **Know standardized tests commonly used in ESL programs in Texas and know how to interpret their results**

The state of Texas uses different standardized tests to provide an accurate measure of student achievement in reading, writing, mathematics, science, and social studies. Subsequent test performance results are used as a gauge for district and school accountability.

STAAR Tests

The **State of Texas Assessments of Academic Readiness (STAAR)** testing program includes the following tests:

- **STAAR:** State of Texas Assessments of Academic Readiness is for all students who do not qualify for one of the other STAAR assessments.

- **STAAR Spanish:** State of Texas Assessments of Academic Readiness Spanish is for ELLs in grades 3–5 whose **Language Proficiency Assessment Committee (LPAC)**, in collaboration with the **Admission, Review, and Dismissal (ARD)** committee, finds that the student needs special education services.

- **STAAR L:** State of Texas Assessments of Academic Readiness L is for ELLs who were first enrolled in grades 3–9 in 2011–12 and who meet requirements for the linguistically accommodated version. In some situations the LPAC, in collaboration with the ARD committee, may also play a role in this decision if the child also receives special education services.

- **STAAR Modified:** State of Texas Assessments of Academic Readiness Modified is for ELLs who were first enrolled in grades 3–9 in 2011–12 and are receiving special education services with a disability that significantly affects academic progress. This is an ARD decision with LPAC collaboration if the student is also an ELL.

- **STAAR Alternate:** State of Texas Assessments of Academic Readiness Alternate is for students in grades 3–8 and high school who receive special education services due to significant cognitive disabilities. This is an ARD decision with LPAC collaboration if the student is an ELL.

- **End-of-Course Exams:** Currently, End-of-Course (EOC) exams are given for English I, English II, Algebra I, biology, and U.S. history. However, these are subject to change as the state is reevaluating frequency and topics of the EOC exams.

(Adapted from the State of Texas Assessments of Academic Readiness Assessments Comparison Chart for the 2012–13 academic year)

Remember that testing requirements are frequently modified or updated. It is important to periodically review the latest guidelines posted on the state's education website. For further information, refer to www.tea.state.tx.us/student.assessment/staar/ and the STAAR assessment comparison chart located on the main page.

TELPAS Levels

The Texas English Language Proficiency Assessment System (TELPAS) assesses the English language proficiency of K-12 ELLs or LEPs in compliance with the **No Child Left Behind (NCLB) Act** in the domains of speaking, reading, listening, and writing in English. As an annual assessment, TELPAS provides data that indicate an ELL's progress, not mastery of content with a pass or fail score.

Aligned with the Texas English Language Proficiency Standards (ELPS), TELPAS is administered each spring to all ELLs, including those who are not participating in a bilingual or ESL program. The continuous data from one academic year to the next provide an annual look at a student's progress in English language development.

Students' progress is measured into four proficiency levels: beginning, intermediate, advanced, and advanced high.

1. **Beginning:** The beginning rating is for students who are in the early stages of learning English, unable to maintain conversations, and rely on using words or phrases they have memorized.

2. **Intermediate:** The intermediate rating is for students who are able to use common, basic English in an academic setting and are able to communicate socially about familiar topics while understanding most of simple conversations. However, these students still require extensive English language support to comprehend what they are learning.

3. **Advanced:** The advanced rating is for students who are able to use academic or concept language in classroom settings when they receive some English language support. Socially these students understand most of what is spoken, but they still struggle with unfamiliar grammar and vocabulary.

4. **Advanced high:** The advanced-high rating is for students who use academic or concept English with little, if any, English language support, even when presented with unfamiliar materials. These students are able to communicate clearly and fluently in social situations.

(Adapted from the 2012 Texas Student Assessment Program Interpreting Assessment Reports document)

Additional information and specifics can be found at www.tea.state.tx.us/student. assessment/ell/telpas/.

SKILL 7.4   **Know state-mandated Limited English Proficient (LEP) policies, including the role of the Language Proficiency Assessment Committee (LPAC), and procedures for implementing LPAC recommendations for LEP identification, placement, and exit**

Limited English Proficient (LEP) Policies

Title VII of the Improving America's School's Act of 1994 defines an LEP as one who

(A)
- Was not born in the U.S., or whose native language is a language other than English and comes from an environment where a language other than English is dominant, or is a native American or Alaska native or who is a resident of the outlying areas and comes from an environment where a language other than English has had a significant impact on the individual's development of English

- Is migratory and whose native language is other than English and comes from an environment where a language other than English is dominant

(B)
- Has sufficient difficulty speaking, reading, writing, or understanding the English language that those difficulties may deny such individual the opportunity to learn successfully in classrooms where the language of instruction is English, or to participate fully in our society

When the evaluation of LEP students with disabilities is under consideration, the ARD committee in conjunction with the LPAC is charged with making assessment and accommodation decisions for students. The ARD committee and the LPAC must ensure that issues related to the student's special education needs and language proficiency are carefully considered.

Language Proficiency Assessment Committee (LPAC)

Each public school or academic facility that services ELLs must have a Language Proficiency Assessment Committee. This committee may consist of administrators, teachers, and community representatives. The committee monitors the academic needs and progress of ELLs and oversees assessment and accommodation decisions on a per-student basis, basing decisions upon state procedures and requirements. Should the child also receive special education services, then the ARD committee will work with the LPAC to make state assessment decisions for STAAR, TELPAS, and TEKS.

Whenever an educator has a question or concern about an ELL's educational placement, the LPAC can provide historical background information about the student, as well as help make decisions for future interventions and testing procedures.

For further information on the role of the LPAC: http://www.tea.state.tx.us/student. assessment/ell/lpac/.

SKILL 7.5 Understand relationships among state-mandated standards, instruction, and assessment in the ESL classroom

The Role of the STAAR Program

The State of Texas Assessments of Academic Readiness (STAAR) testing program replaced the **Texas Assessment of Knowledge and Skills (TAKS)** in 2012. STAAR places more emphasis on the integration of the state curriculum, classroom instruction, and state-mandated assessment. The testing program is aligned with Texas Essential Knowledge and Skills (TEKS) curriculum and is created to measure students' progress and acquisition of the TEKS.

The STAAR program assesses grades 3-8 in reading and mathematics, grades 4 and 7 in writing, grades 5 and 8 in science, and grade 8 in social studies. There are various forms of STAAR available for students in general education, special education, or English language learning. These accommodations have state guidelines that must be met before receiving permission to implement.

The STAAR program is more rigorous than the TAKS assessment, emphasizing readiness standards that are considered necessary for grade-level success as well as supporting standards necessary for preparation for the next grade level. Each STAAR question may address two or more TEKS objectives and are complex in construction, often requiring students to synthesize information from a given passage or content information and complete two or more steps to solve a problem while using deductive and logical reasoning.

(Adapted from Texas State's media toolkit at www.tea.state.tx.us/index2.aspx?id= 2147504081)

For additional information, refer to the Texas Education Agency's website at: http://www.tea.state.tx.us/student.assessment/staar/.

ELPS Descriptions

The English Language Proficiency Standards (ELPS) provide the proficiency level descriptions and ELL's expectations of the English language. There is a direct connection between the ELPS and the TELPAS-tested levels of English proficiency in reading, writing, speaking, and listening. These proficiency levels are not grade-specific as ELLs may have different proficiency levels within the domains.

It is required that school districts identify the student's English language proficiency levels and implement the ELPS, combining them with the state of Texas TEKS for each subject in the required curriculum. When the ELPS are combined with the state of Texas TEKS, it creates a linguistically accommodated instruction with language supports that make academic content accessible to ELLs.

It is recommended that the ESL teacher becomes familiar with the ELPS and its use in the classroom. The following websites provide comprehensive information.

- For a detailed look at the ELPS and the proficiency levels: www.esc4.net/docs/122-ELPS.pdf

- Supporting State of Texas document and outline of the ELPS: http://ritter.tea.state.tx.us/rules/tac/chapter074/ch074a.html#74.4

SKILL 7.6 **Know how to use ongoing assessment to plan and adjust instruction that addresses individual student needs and enables ESL students to achieve learning goals**

A basic premise of assessment is "test what you teach." In the high-stakes testing of today, teachers are expected to show good results with the exit tests of their students. Teachers can use regular classroom testing to determine and monitor each student's strengths and weaknesses. By aligning instruction of the ELLs with the curriculum, the instructor can plan reinforcement of deficit skills as needed. This system is effective in preventing problems later when more complex skills are introduced. By integrating language skills into the content area at all times, the instructor can make the language classroom a motivating place, with many opportunities for further learning.

Assessment is diagnostic and ongoing, whereas *evaluation* is used to judge students' learning (Cobb, 2003: in Tompkins, 2009). Authentic assessment tools and tests give a more complete picture of what the student knows about the subject matter as well as the strategies and skills they use, whereas tests compare student performance against grade-level standards (Wilson, Martens & Arya, 2005: in Tompkins, 2009).

Teachers can use the information gathered from their testing in different ways (Chapman & Snyder, 2000):

- Tests can be used to orient and slant teaching practices in desirable ways.
- Teachers can be motivated to improve their teaching.
- Testing gives information for remedial work.

In the case of students demonstrating possible learning difficulties, the classroom teacher will have preliminary diagnostics with which to recommend further testing.

DOMAIN III   FOUNDATIONS OF ESL EDUCATION, CULTURAL
                    AWARENESS, AND FAMILY AND COMMUNITY
                    INVOLVEMENT

COMPETENCY 8

THE ESL TEACHER UNDERSTANDS THE FOUNDATIONS OF ESL EDUCATION AND TYPES
OF ESL PROGRAMS

SKILL 8.1   **Know the historical, theoretical, and policy foundations of ESL
             education, and use this knowledge to plan, implement, and advocate
             for effective ESL programs**

Several legal precedents have established that schools must provide equal educational
opportunities for ELLs. This series has led directly to improved language instruction and
accommodations for language deficiencies.

Civil Rights Act of 1964

The Civil Rights Act of 1964 established that schools, as recipients of federal funds,
cannot discriminate against ELLs:

> No person in the United States shall, on the grounds of race, color, or
> national origin, be excluded from participation in, be denied the benefits
> of, or be subjected to discrimination under any program or activity
> receiving Federal financial assistance.

In 1970, this mandate was detailed more specifically for ELLs in the *May 25
Memorandum:*

> Where inability to speak and understand the English language excludes
> national origin-minority group children from effective participation in the
> educational program offered by a school district, the district must take
> affirmative steps to rectify the language deficiency in order to open its
> instructional program to these students.

The memorandum specifically addressed the practice of placing ELLs, based on their
English language skills, in classes with mentally retarded students; excluding them from
college preparatory classes; and notifying parents of ELLs of school activities, even if
translation is required.

Lau v. Nichols and *Castaneda v. Pickard*

In 1974 the Supreme Court offered a unanimous ruling in *Lau v. Nichols* that established the Lau Plan, providing specific requirements that schools must fulfill:

- Meet legal criteria for programming
- Form/convene a Language Assessment Committee
- Outline staff responsibilities and credentials for instruction
- Identify assessment/evaluative tools for ongoing assessment
- Set program criteria (entrance/exit standards)
- Set parameters for ELL transition and monitoring
- Determine program effectiveness

Schools could no longer merely provide students with the same facilities, textbooks, teachers, and curriculum as other students have available. In this ruling, the Supreme Court recognized that students who do not understand English are effectively excluded from any meaningful education.

In a later decision, *Castaneda v. Pickard* (filed in 1978 but not settled until 1981), a federal court established three specific criteria that schools must use to determine the effectiveness of bilingual education programs:

1. A program for English language learners must be based on pedagogically sound educational theory that is recognized by experts in the field.

2. The program must be implemented effectively with resources provided for personnel, instructional materials, and space.

3. The program must produce results that indicate the language barrier is being overcome.

A Nation at Risk Report

The 1983 *A Nation at Risk* report, produced by the National Commission on Excellence in Education, concluded that the U.S. educational system was failing to meet the national need for a competitive workforce. This prompted a flurry of education reforms and initiated the National Assessment of Educational Progress (NAEP), which keeps an ongoing record of school performance. While general participation is voluntary, all schools that receive Title I money must participate. This includes every public school serving low socioeconomic and minority students, which includes a large percentage of ELLs.

No Child Left Behind Act

The No Child Left Behind Act of 2001 established requirements that school districts must meet to continue to receive federal funds. The NCLB Act has a number of requirements, but the one that has affected ELLs the most is the system of evaluating school performance based on disaggregated data. Schools can no longer rely on high-performing students to average out the low performance of language-challenged students. Although the law is far from perfect, it prohibits schools from burying the low performance of any subpopulation in a school-wide average.

Some issues of concern to educators are the following:

- Increasing the length of the school day and year (U.S. students currently spend 180 days in school compared to Japan with 243, South Korea 220, Israel with 216, Luxembourg 216, and The Netherlands, Scotland, and Thailand with 200)
- Improving student achievement
- Georgia school improvement program
- High-stakes testing
- Improving early childhood education
- Improving teacher quality
- Improving the retention rate of high school dropouts
- Making higher education affordable for everyone
- Using educational technology in the classroom
- International Baccalaureate programs
- Teaching technology in the classroom
- Staff development programs that provide insight into teaching ESL learners (these programs are meant not only for ESL staff but for teachers across subject areas)

SKILL 8.2   **Know types of ESL programs (e.g., self-contained, pull-out, newcomer centers, dual-language, and immersion), their characteristics, their goals, and research findings on their effectiveness**

The major models of ESL programs differ depending on the sources consulted. However, general consensus recognizes the following program models with different instructional methods.

Immersion Education Models

In immersion programs, instruction is initiated in the student's nonnative language, using the second language as the medium of instruction for both academic content and the second language. Two of these models strive for full bilingualism: one is for language-majority students and the other is for language minorities.

English Language Development (ELD) or ESL Pull-Out

ELD or ESL pull-out programs include various approaches to teaching English to nonnative speakers. In 1997 TESOL standards defined these approaches by an intent to teach the ELL to communicate in social settings, engage in academic tasks, and use

English in socially and culturally appropriate ways. The following are three well-known approaches to ELD or ESL:

- **Grammar-based ESL:** Instruction *about* the language, stressing its structure, functions, and vocabulary through rules, drills, and error correction.

- **Communication-based ESL:** Instruction in English that emphasizes *using* the language in meaningful contexts. There is little stress on correctness in the early stages and more emphasis on comprehensible input in the early stages to foster communication and lower anxiety when risk-taking.

- **Content-based ESL:** Instruction in English that attempts to develop language skills and prepare ELLs to study grade-level content material in English. Emphasis on language, but with graded introduction to content areas, vocabulary, and basic concepts.

Structured English Immersion

The goal of a structured English immersion program is English proficiency. ELLs receive structured instruction in English so that subject matter is comprehensible. This program is with sizeable groups of ELLs who speak the same language and are in the same grade level or with a diverse population of language-minority students. There is little or no L1 language support. Teachers use sheltered instructional techniques and have strong receptive skills in the students' native or heritage language.

Submersion with Primary Language Support

The goal of submersion with primary language support is English proficiency. Bilingual teachers or aides support the minority students in each grade level who are ELLs. In small groups, the ELLs are tutored by reviewing the content areas in their primary language. Teachers use the L1 to support English content classes; ELLs achieve limited literacy in L1.

Canadian French Immersion

The targeted population of a Canadian French immersion program includes language-majority students. The goal is for all students of the majority language (English) to become fluent in L2 (French). The students are immersed in the L2 for the first two years using sheltered language instruction and then English L1 is introduced.

Indigenous-Language Immersion

An indigenous-language immersion program focuses on endangered languages, such as Navajo. The goal is bilingualism; the program is socially, linguistically, and cognitively attuned to the native culture and community context. This method supports endangered minority languages and develops academic skills in minority language and culture as well as in the English language and predominant culture.

Self-Contained

The self-contained program consists of monolingual English instruction using ESL methods to teach oral and written English and to foster cognitive development. This is a strategic option for schools not staffed with a sufficient number of bilingual teachers. An ESL classroom instructs students in English but remains sensitive to their home language and culture.

Newcomer Centers

Newcomer centers are designed to temporarily help students who are new to the U.S. adjust to both the educational system and the social environment. These centers and programs differ tremendously in their structure and set-up. Some are part of the regular school system and others are self-contained. Although the centers are an ad-hoc response to local education needs, they share a dedication to helping LEP newcomer students transition to the American school system as quickly as possible, and also share an educational approach that recognizes the importance of acquiring English language skills as just one of the skills necessary in the transition process.

Characteristics of Effective Programs

Research findings suggest that there are several characteristics of effective programs for language minority groups:

- Supportive whole-school contexts

- High expectations for language minority groups supported by active learning environments that are academically challenging

- Intensive staff development programs designed to assist ALL teachers in providing effective instruction to language-minority students

- Expert instructional leaders and teachers

- Emphasis on functional communication between teacher and students and among fellow students

- Organization of the instruction of basic skills and academic content around thematic units

- Frequent student interaction through the use of collaborative learning techniques

- Teachers with a high commitment of the educational success of all their students

- Principals supportive of their instructional staff and of teacher autonomy while maintaining an awareness of district policies on curriculum and academic accountability

- Involvement of majority and minority parents in formal parent support activities

(Adapted from Rennie, 1993)

SKILL 8.3 **Apply knowledge of the various types of ESL programs to make appropriate instruction and management decisions**

Many types of programs can be effective. The choice should be made by local authorities and communities after serious consideration of the students' needs and available resources.

Certain factors, including demographics, student characteristics, and resources, will most likely have considerable influence on the decision of the authorities and a community when selecting an effective program model.

- **District or school demographics:** Some school districts have large minority populations of a single-language background, whereas others may have a few students from as many as 100 home languages. Factors such as the total number of language minority students, the number of students from each language background, and their distribution across grades and schools will affect the type of program needed to aid district students (McKeon, 1987).

- **Student characteristics:** Student populations may differ because of educational factors present in their home countries before arriving in the U.S. Many students may have little or no academic preparation while others may be equal or surpass their peers in the U.S.

- **District or school resources:** School districts with the infrastructure to deal with significant language minorities have teachers, aides, and administrators trained to work with ELLs. They may have a strong community pool of bilingual personnel with which to staff bilingual programs. Other school districts may have serious problems in these areas when faced with a sudden influx of students from one or more unfamiliar language backgrounds.

Material resources also influence the type of program chosen. Some districts may have difficulty in finding classrooms for pull-out programs while others with declining enrollment may be able to accommodate magnet or ESL resource centers (McKeon, 1987).

SKILL 8.4   **Apply knowledge of research findings related to ESL education, including research on instructional and management practices in ESL programs, to assist in planning and implementing effective ESL programs**

The following language-learning theories support specific instructional strategies.

Theory 1

If the instructional environment for L2 learners is characterized by high expectations for speaking correctly, total memorization of grammatical rules and vocabulary, as well as constant error correction, the L2 learner will quickly lose motivation to continue the learning process.

Strategy: Total Physical Response

A "command-driven" instructional technique developed by psychologist James Asher, TPR is a useful tool in the early developmental stage of second-language acquisition, as well as for LEP students without any previous exposure to English. The main tenet of TPR is that input is very comprehensible, in the form of commands and gestures and is also fun for the L2 learner. Asher supports this theory with the idea that the process mirrors the process that young children use when acquiring their primary language: children gradually develop both their awareness and attempts to communicate, until listening comprehension skills have reached a comfortable level. At this point, the child will begin to speak. Through TPR, instructors interact with students by way of commands/gestures, and the students respond with a physical response. TPR emphasizes listening rather than speaking; and, students are encouraged to speak only when they feel ready.

Theory 2

In order for the L2 learner to begin production in the target language, the following principles must be observed and implemented:

- During the silent period (when learners listen, instead of speaking), the instructors must use comprehensible input, corresponding to the learners' level of understanding in the target language.

- Attempts to speak and produce language, on the part of the L2 learner, will gradually occur.

- The class curriculum must be aligned with specific speech production skills—that is, instead of using a linear-grammatical approach, instruction should be topically centered, such as nonsequential lessons on weather, things found in a house, how to tell time, and so on.

Strategy: The Natural Approach

T. Terrell and S. Krashen are the researchers behind the comprehensive Natural Approach. The underlying assumption is that any learner of any age has the ability to receive comprehensible speech input and determine its pattern without someone else having to spell it out for them.

According to Terrell and Krashen, the approach involves large amounts of comprehensible input, whether it is situational, from visual aids or cues, or grammatical. This input is respectful of "the initial preproduction period, expecting speech to emerge not from artificial practice, but from motivated language use, progressing from early single-word responses up to more and more coherent discourse" (Celce-Murcia, 1991). Terrell also maintains that being grammatically correct is not as important as the learner enjoying the learning process. Critics of Terrell maintain that by not correcting the learner's errors early on, fluency is achieved at the expense of accuracy.

Theory 3

When learners are instructed through content-based instruction (CBI) such as mathematics, science, social studies, and so on, they tend to achieve a much higher proficiency level in the target language than if they were only instructed in the target language through other ESL methods.

Strategy: The Cognitive Academic Language Learning Approach

The **Cognitive Academic Language Learning Approach (CALLA)** is the brainchild of Chamot and O'Malley (1994). Their work is based on the principle that the child learns far more language in content classes than in ESL pull-out classes.

CALLA integrates language development, content-area instruction, and explicit instruction in learning strategies. It includes the following tenets:

- The L2 learners' actual grade level in the main subject areas of mathematics, science, and social studies, and so on should be the deciding factor for content.

- The L2 learners should be exposed to and gradually acquire the specific language used when studying in the subject areas, such as: Add this column of numbers, Determine x in this algebraic problem, Identify the properties of this cell.

- The L2 learners should be encouraged to use higher-level cognitive processes, such as application, analysis, and synthesis.

COMPETENCY 9

THE ESL TEACHER UNDERSTANDS FACTORS THAT AFFECT ESL STUDENTS' LEARNING AND IMPLEMENTS STRATEGIES FOR CREATING AN EFFECTIVE MULTICULTURAL AND MULTILINGUAL LEARNING ENVIRONMENT

SKILL 9.1   **Understand cultural and linguistic diversity in ESL classrooms and other factors that may affect students' learning of academic content, language, and culture (e.g., age, developmental characteristics, academic strengths and needs, preferred learning styles, personality, sociocultural factors, home environment, attitude, exceptionalities)**

Although there is a continuous effort to establish a "standard" English to be taught to ELLs, English learning and acquisition depends on the cultural and linguistic background of the ELL as well as preconceived perceptions of English language cultural influences. These factors can act as a filter, causing confusion and inhibiting learning. Since language by definition is an attempt to share knowledge, the cultural, ethnic, and linguistic diversity of learners influences both their own history and the way they approach and learn a new language.

Teachers must assess the ELL to determine how cultural, ethnic, and linguistic experience can impact the student's learning. This evaluation should take into account many factors, including

- The cultural background and educational sophistication of the ELL
- The exposure of the ELL to various English language variants and cultural beliefs

No single approach, program, or set of practices fits all students' needs, backgrounds, and experiences. For example, the ideal program for a Native American teenager attending an isolated tribal school may fail to reach a Hispanic youth enrolled in an inner city or suburban district.

The ELL's Cultural Background

Culture encompasses the sum of human activity and symbolic structures that have significance and importance for a particular group of people. Culture is manifested in language, customs, beliefs, institutions, history, arts, and other representative characteristics, and is a means of understanding the lives and actions of people.

Customs

Customs play an important part in language learning because they directly affect interpersonal exchanges. What is polite in one culture might be offensive in another.

For example, in European American culture, making direct eye contact is considered polite and not to make eye contact connotes deviousness, inattention, or rude behavior.

The custom in many Asian and Native American cultures is exactly the opposite. Teachers who are unaware of this cultural difference can easily offend an Asian ELL and unwittingly cause a barrier to learning. However, teachers who are familiar with this custom can make efforts not to offend the learner and can teach the difference between the two customs so that the ELL can learn how to interact without allowing contrary customs to interfere.

Beliefs and Institutions

Beliefs and institutions have a strong emotional influence on ELLs. They should always be respected. Whereas customs should be adaptable—similar to switching registers when speaking—no effort should be made to change the beliefs or institutional values of an ELL. Even though the beliefs and values of different cultures often have irreconcilable differences, they should be addressed. In these instances, teachers must respect alternative attitudes and adopt an "agree to disagree" attitude.

Presenting new ideas and contrasting points of view is a part of growth, learning, and understanding, and should not be avoided. However, all presentations should be neutral, and no effort should be made to alter a learner's thinking. While addressing individual cultural differences, teachers should also teach tolerance of all cultures. This attitude is especially important in a culturally diverse classroom, but will also serve all students well in their future interactions.

History and Art

Studying the history and various art forms of a culture reveals much about the culture and offers opportunities to tap into the interests and talents of ELLs. Comparing the history and art of different cultures encourages critical thinking and often reveals commonalities as well as differences, leading to greater understanding among people.

How Culture Affects Language Learning

Culture constitutes a rich component of language learning. It offers a means of drawing learners into the learning process and greatly expands their understanding of a new culture, as well as their own. Second-language acquisition, according to the findings of Saville-Troike (1986), places the learner in the position of having to learn a second culture. The outcome of learning a second culture can have negative or positive results, depending on not only how teaching is approached, but also outside factors. How people in the new culture respond to ELLs makes them feel welcome or rejected.

The attitudes and behavior of the learner's family are particularly important. If the family is supportive and embraces the second culture, then the effect is typically positive. However, if acculturation is perceived as rejecting the primary culture, then the child risks feeling alienated from both cultures.

There are many different ways that students are affected by the **cultural differences** in their native culture and home when compared with the culture being acquired through schooling and daily life in a foreign culture. The following points, adapted from Peregoy and Boyle (2008), illustrate some of the ways that culture affects us daily and thus affect students in their participation, learning, and adjustment to a different society and its schools.

- **Family structures:** What constitutes a family? What are the rights and responsibilities of each family member? What is the hierarchy of authority?

- **Life cycles:** What are the criteria for defining stages, periods, or transitions in life? What rites of passage are there? What behaviors are considered appropriate for children of different ages? How might these conflict with behaviors taught or encouraged in school?

- **Gender roles and interpersonal relationships:** How do the roles of girls and women differ from those of boys and men? Which behaviors are considered socially acceptable for boys versus girls at different ages? How do people greet each other? Do girls work and interact with boys? Is deference shown, and to whom and by whom?

- **Discipline:** What is discipline? Who or what is considered responsible if a child misbehaves? The child? Parents? Older siblings? The environment? Is blame even ascribed? Who has authority over whom? How is behavior traditionally controlled? To what extent and in what domains?

- **Time and space:** How important is punctuality? How important is speed in completing a task? How much space are people accustomed to? What significance is associated with different cultural locations or directions, including north, south, east, and west?

- **Religion:** What restrictions are there on topics discussed in school? Are dietary restrictions to be observed, including fasting? What restrictions are associated with death and the dead?

- **Food:** What is eaten? In what order and how often is food eaten? Which foods are restricted? Which foods are typical? What social obligations are there with regard to food giving, reciprocity, and honoring people? What restrictions or proscriptions are associated with handling, offering, or discarding food?

- **Health and hygiene:** How are illnesses treated and by whom? What is to be considered the cause? If a student were involved in an accident at school, would any of the common first aid practices be unacceptable?

- **History, traditions, and holidays:** Which events and people are sources of pride for this group? To what extent does the group in the United States identify with the history and traditions of the country of origin? What holidays and celebrations are considered appropriate for observing in school? Which ones are appropriate for private observance?

- **Age:** Age can impact second-language acquisition when a culture determines what a person does, as well as when they can do it. For example, middle-class European Americans tend to expect that children will play and behave appropriately for their age, rather than take on adult responsibilities. In contrast, young Cree Indian children are expected to carry out many adult responsibilities. Furthermore, many Cree parents disapprove of academic activities because they distract the children from involvement in the Cree society.

SKILL 9.2   **Know how to create an effective multicultural and multilingual learning environment that addresses the affective, linguistic, and cognitive needs of ESL students and facilitates students' learning and language acquisition**

Language study using authentic language, and the uses of language have become the watchwords in language acquisition. Theorists now believe that language use is the proper goal of language studies and that it should be studied *in context* instead of in isolated sentences that provide examples of only a specific grammar point or structure. In the move away from decontextualized, graded textbooks, researchers encourage the study of discourse above the sentence level.

Teachers need to provide a wide range of materials, including educational technology (such as videos, computers, DVDs, and electronic tablets) to create a language-rich environment, believed to be the key to comprehensible input and high motivation.

And finally, all four language skills—listening, speaking, reading, and writing—should be practiced at all levels. One way of achieving the practice of all four skills, while using authentic language, is to incorporate task-based activities into the instruction.

SKILL 9.3   **Know factors that contribute to cultural bias (e.g., stereotyping, prejudice, ethnocentrism) and know how to create a culturally responsive learning environment**

Many factors might contribute to cultural bias. It is important to understand these factors in order to know how to create a positive learning environment for ELLs.

Cultural Bias Factors

The terms **stereotyping, prejudice, discrimination, racism,** and **ethnocentrism** are often confused. A teacher should know their distinctions in order to both confront his or her own potential biases and to make students in the classroom aware of these issues.

- Stereotyping is attributing false or exaggerated characteristics of a group to an individual.

- Prejudice is a prejudgment or an unjustified attitude toward an individual based solely on his or her membership in a group.

- Discrimination is a negative behavior or treatment that a person shows when he or she is prejudiced against another person or group.

- Racism is discrimination based on race.

- Ethnocentrism is the belief in the superiority of one culture over another.

Creating a Positive Learning Environment

In order for language-minority students to learn English, a secure, positive, and motivating language-learning environment must be provided. How schools meet these criteria depends on the individual school and its district.

A positive learning environment results when the school provides a safe and attractive atmosphere, free of prejudices. The school should also be one in which administrators and instructors exact high expectations for linguistically and culturally appropriate learning experiences from the student body. The teachers, administrators, and other staff should be trained to prepare instructional materials and other services specifically for language-minority students.

The school should be a place where language-minority parents and their input are welcomed, since they are the at-home primary teachers of their children. Parents should be informed of decisions affecting their children, their schools, and school districts.

Strategies for providing a safe and secure environment may include assigning a buddy from the same country or language group as the ELL to go with the newcomer during the day and show him or her such essential things as where the bathroom and cafeteria are, how to line up and receive food in the cafeteria, and how to eat specific foods in the cafeteria.

Another strategy is to follow *predictable routines* in the classroom. Predictability is important for all students, but especially ELLs and those whose lives may have been in turmoil for some time.

Placing new students in the center or front section of the classroom is another way to integrate them into the mainstream of activities even if they do not speak a word of English. If groups are used in the classroom, the new ELLs should be placed in a group that remains stable for a long period of time to establish a mini-community of interdependence.

SKILL 9.4   **Demonstrate sensitivity to students' diverse cultural and socioeconomic backgrounds and show respect for language differences**

Teaching ELLs is a rewarding profession. Often, however, because of their own lack of understanding of cultural manifestations, teachers unwittingly cause barriers to language learning by offending their students without knowing that they have done so. Therefore, all teachers who are involved in the education of ELLs need to learn as much as they can about the ELL's culture.

Demonstrating Cultural Sensitivity

Teaching Journals

Teachers are participants as well as observers in their classrooms. As such, they are in a unique position to observe what makes their students uncomfortable. By writing these observations in a teaching journal, the teacher can begin to note what activities and topics make the students in her classroom uncomfortable. Does this discomfort come from multicultural insensitivity?

Appropriate Wait Time

The wait time for student responses varies in different cultures. The average amount of wait time in American classrooms is less than that in many other cultures. Students who are struggling to formulate their answers may need more time than the teacher normally gives for responding. Also, if the questions are rhetorical, students may be reluctant to answer them, as they see no point to such a question. Teachers should do the following:

- Allow students to express their thoughts fully without interruption.
- Allow students to discuss their answer with a partner before sharing with the whole group.

Balancing Group Work

Cooperative group work is based on the premise that many cultures are more comfortable working in collaborative groups. However, many students may feel that the teacher is the only academic authority in the classroom and as such, should be the only one to answer questions, not their peers. Some students feel more comfortable with different instructional formats than others. This may be due to both cultural and individual preferences. By balancing group work with teacher-directed instruction, both points of view can be accommodated.

Fostering a Respect for Language Differences

Literacy and reading instruction are areas in which multicultural sensitivity can be increased in the classroom regardless of the level of the students. Many immigrant children arrive in the classroom with few, if any, literacy skills. They may not have had the opportunity to go to school. Others may be fully literate, with substantial prior education. In both cases, reading materials that are culturally sensitive are necessary for the students, both native English speakers and ELLs, to have the opportunity to discuss the ways in which different cultures are alike and different. Oral discussions of the books will provide opportunities for comprehensible input and negotiation of meaning.

Research has shown that the key to any reading program is extensive reading (Day & Bamford, 1998; Krashen & Terrell, 1983). Advantages include building vocabulary and background knowledge, as well as interest in reading and comprehension. For the multicultural classroom, it is important to provide culturally sensitive materials. Avoid materials that distort or omit certain historical events, portray stereotyping, contain loaded words, use speech that is culturally inaccurate, portray gender roles, elders, and family inaccurately, or distort or offend a student's self-image. All materials should be of high literary quality.

Show and tell is another strategy for raising awareness of the richness of other cultures. Students of all ages can bring in objects from their home culture and tell the class about their uses, where they are from, how they are made, and so on.

Misunderstandings can be discussed in the classroom by asking students to share an incident that involved cultural misunderstanding. Questions can be asked about the nature of the misunderstanding—what was involved: words, body language, social customs, or stereotypes.

SKILL 9.5   Apply strategies for creating among students an awareness of and respect for linguistic and cultural diversity

Racism, stereotyping, and discrimination are difficult social issues to address in the classroom, because they are cultural elements that die hard. Even so, teachers are charged with addressing these issues in the classroom, especially when they carry negative connotations. Encouraging an all-inclusive classroom climate in which everyone is an equal is a start. This is fairly easy when dealing with young children, but with older students, the movie *The Ron Clark Story* (2006) could be used to initiate a discussion of these themes. The movie shows how an idealistic young teacher from North Carolina deals with the problems of racism, stereotyping, and discrimination in his New York City classroom.

Language rights refer to the right of each individual to enjoy the uniquely individual and communal privilege of belonging to a language group in which human beings appreciate the world and one another (Kramsch, 1998: 77). ELLs often feel as if they lose a part of themselves when faced with the complexities of learning a new language and culture. To lessen these feelings of alienation and isolation, including elements of the ELL's culture and previous knowledge enhances the learning in the English classroom.

Including culture study in the classroom may be achieved by having each student do a research project on his or her culture and report back to the class. Culture studies of this nature promote reading, writing, speaking, learning to give presentations, and creating visuals. Should there be more than one student from the same culture, pairs or small groups could be organized. Alternative types of assessment could be used to evaluate the process.

COMPETENCY 10

THE ESL TEACHER KNOWS HOW TO SERVE AS AN ADVOCATE FOR ESL STUDENTS AND FACILITATE FAMILY AND COMMUNITY INVOLVEMENT IN THEIR EDUCATION

SKILL 10.1   **Apply knowledge of effective strategies advocating educational and social equity for ESL students (e.g., participating in LPAC and ARD meetings, serving on SBDM committees, serving as a resource for teachers)**

Texas law requires a **Site-Based Decision Making (SBDM)** committee at the school district level as well as at each local school campus. ESL instructors can use participation in such committees to advocate for English language learners. By advocating for the ELL, the ESL instructor can ensure that students in his or her charge are able to participate in the school band, science club, math club, chess club, sports teams, and all other activities in which students of their age and inclination participate.

Encouraging students and their families to make full use of public resources such as the local public library—including its online resources—will help them expand their own knowledge and understanding of resources available to English-language learners. In addition, many libraries have afterschool, Saturday, or holiday programs to encourage constructive use of students' time.

Museums, too, often have educational outreach programs that can be extremely beneficial. Other resources such as parks and the local YMCA and YWCA (or similar organizations) offer recreational and skill-building facilities to local residents.

SKILL 10.2   **Understand the importance of family involvement in the education of ESL students and know how to facilitate parent/guardian participation in their children's education and school activities**

Parents and other family members often delight in being part of the educational community when encouraged to do so. Schools that encourage all stakeholders in the community to participate in the school system have strong community resources upon which to draw when (and if) problems occur.

Facilitation by the ESL instructor can help get family members involved. Through outreach, for example:

- Older members of the community can be encouraged to mentor at-risk students.

- Parents and grandparents can serve as tutors for students with academic difficulties.

- Room parents provide support for the many classroom events throughout the school year.

- Parent-teacher organizations (PTOs) enable family members with organizational and financial skills to serve the school community.

Remember that a little effort often goes a long way. Invitations to relatives of ELLs to talk about their homeland and culture is an excellent way to encourage otherwise reticent parents to get involved in their school.

SKILL 10.3   Apply skills for communicating and collaborating effectively with the parents/guardians of ESL students in a variety of educational contexts

Often in schools, parents, grandparents, and other people involved in children's lives want to take a more active role in the educational process. They also all seem to have an opinion on the appropriate method for teaching students how to read. Sometimes this can lead to controversy and misunderstandings.

It is important to provide opportunities for parents to come into the school and participate in activities to encourage their participation in the schooling of their children. During these programs, it is just as important to share tidbits of information about the methodologies and strategies being implemented. In this way, the public can begin to understand the differences in ESL instruction today, in comparison to what it may have been in their native cultures when they attended school. The perceived difference is often the biggest statement of concern made by adults concerning current educational trends.

Educating Family Members

Taking the time to educate parents and other family members not only helps to enhance understanding and open communication; it can also provide more support for students than the school alone would ever be able to provide.

Some strategies for educating parents and family members are

- Parent workshops offered on various topics
- Newsletter pieces or paragraphs
- Individual parent meetings

- Inviting parents to observe lessons
- Information shared during social times when parents are invited into the school
- Bingo games in which the correct answer on the Bingo board is a fact about English language instruction

Maintaining Communication

It is important to share both general information about English language instruction and specific information about students with parents and school personnel. Once the teacher has gathered sufficient information on the students, he or she must find appropriate methods to share this information with those who need the data. Again, depending on the audience, the amount and type of information shared may vary. Some ways to share information with parents or guardians include:

- Individual parent meetings
- Small group meetings
- Regular parent updates through phone calls
- Charts and graphs of progress sent home
- Notes sent home

SKILL 10.4 **Know how community members and resources can positively affect student learning in the ESL program and be able to access community resources to enhance the education of ESL students**

Inviting guest speakers or even simply talking about role models are great ways of enhancing the ELL's educational experience. When the ESL teacher is able to point out resources and community members who have "made it," motivation to succeed is increased.

One of the most promising pieces of legislation to support ELLs' learning and achievement is the proposed "DREAM Act" (Development, Relief and Education of Alien Minors Act). The Dream Act was introduced in the U.S. Congress on March 26, 2009. This federal legislation would provide the opportunity to alien minors the opportunity to earn conditional permanent residency if they graduate from U.S. high schools, are of good moral character, and have been in the country continuously for five years or more prior to the bill's enactment.

Various community organizations provide scholarships to children of different heritages for the advancement of their education. These scholarships can make a huge difference to ELLs.

GLOSSARY OF ABBREVIATIONS AND ACRONYMS

AAPPL (ACTFL Assessment of Performance toward Proficiency in Languages): a language proficiency test maintained by the American Council for the Teaching of Foreign Languages (ACTFL)

ACE (asking, cooperating, empathizing): basic social strategies for second-language acquisition

ARD (Admissions, Review, and Dismissal): a state-mandated committee that makes decisions about the assessment and accommodation of a child who receives special education services

BICS (Basic Interpersonal Communication Skills): a type of language proficiency that ELLs must acquire to function informally in social situations

CALLA (Cognitive Academic Language Learning Approach): a teaching method that helps ELL gain proficiency in their target language by focusing on academic subject matter

CALP (Cognitive Academic Language Proficiency): type of language proficiency that is more demanding than BICS

CBI (content-based instruction): teaching that uses core academic subjects, such as mathematics, social studies, or science, as the foundation for ESL lessons

CUP (Common Underlying Proficiency): skills, ideas, and concepts that ELLs can transfer from their first language to their English learning

DREAM (Development, Relief, and Education of Alien Minors): proposed federal act that would provide the opportunity to alien minors the opportunity to earn conditional permanent residency

ELD (English Language Development): model of English language immersion education

ELL (English language learner): student who is learning the English language in addition to his or her native language

ELPS (English Language Proficiency Standards): standards and levels used to determine ELLs' English language proficiency

EOC (End-of-Course): STAAR exams that measure achievement in specific academic subjects

ESL (English as a Second Language): study of the English language by speakers whose native language is not English

ESOL (English for Speakers of Other Languages): alternative form of the term ESL

IC (instructional conversations): interactive form of initiation and feedback

L1 (first language): an ELL's native language

L2 (second language): an ELL's second language

LAD (Language Acquisition Device): special biological brain mechanism with which all humans are born, as explained in the theory of Noam Chomsky

LEA (Language Experience Approach): teaching approach in which students create a narrative that provides content for instruction

LEP (Limited English Proficient): a government-defined term describing ELLs with restricted access to learning

LET (lowering anxiety, encouragement, taking emotional temperature): basic affective strategies for second-language acquisition

LPAC (Language Proficiency Assessment Committee): state-mandated committee that monitors the academic needs and progress of ELLs and oversees assessment and accommodation decisions

NCLB (No Child Left Behind): federal act of 2001 that established requirements which school districts must meet to continue to receive federal funds

PPP (Presentation, Practice, Production): model in which teachers present small amounts of language to help ELLs acquire communication skills

PRAC (practicing, receiving, analyzing, creating): basic cognitive strategies for second-language acquisition

PTO (parent-teacher organization): a school organization or association (sometimes called PTA) that consists of parents, teachers, and staff members

SBDM (Site-Based Decision Making): state-mandated committee at the school district level as well as at each local school campus

STAAR (State of Texas Assessment of Academic Readiness): program of standardized tests for education in the state of Texas

SVO (subject, verb, object): common sentence structure in the English language

TAKS (Texas Assessment of Knowledge and Skills): former state assessment system replaced in 2012 by STAAR

TEKS (Texas Essential Knowledge and Skills): state standards for Texas K-12 education in public schools

TELPAS (Texas English Language Proficiency Assessment System): exam that tests the proficiency level of each ELL

TOEFL (Test of English as a Foreign Language): language proficiency test used as an entrance exam to U.S. colleges and universities

TPR (Total Physical Response): technique using verbal commands and physical gestures to increase the ELL's oral production

BIBLIOGRAPHY

"2013–2014 LPAC Decision-Making Process for the Texas Assessment Program." *Language Proficiency Assessment Committee (LPAC) Assessment Resources.* Texas Education Agency. 18 Oct. 2013. 2 Jan. 2014. <http://www.tea.state.tx.us/student.assessment/ell/lpac/>

Arreaga-Mayer, C. 1998. "Increasing Active Student Responding and Improving Academic Performance through Classwide Peer Tutoring." *Intervention in School and Clinic* 34: 89–94.

Atkinson, R., and D. Hansen. 1966–67. "Computer-assisted Instruction in Initial Reading: The Stanford Project." *Reading Research Quarterly* 2: 5–26.

Bailey, K. 1983. "Competitiveness and Anxiety in Adult Second Language Learning: Looking at and through the Diary Studies." In: H. W. Seliger and M. H. Long (eds.), *Classroom-Oriented Research in Second Language Acquisition.* Rowley, MA: Newbury House.

Berko Gleason, J. 1993. *The Development of Language.* 3rd ed. NY: Macmillan.

Bermudez, A., and D. Palumbo. 1994. "Bridging the Gap between Literature and Technology: Hypermedia as a Learning Tool for Limited English Proficient Students." *Journal of Educational Issues of Language Minority Students* 14: 165–84.

Bialystok, E., ed. 1991. *Language Processing in Bilingual Children.* Cambridge: CUP.

Blanton, L. L. 1992. "A Holistic Approach to College ESL: Integrating Language and Content." *ELT Journal* 46: 285–93.

Bransford, J. E., and M. K. Johnson. 1972. "Contextual Prerequisites for Understanding: Some Investigations of Comprehension and Recall." *Journal of Verbal Learning and Verbal Behavior* 11: 717–26.

Brown, A. 2008. "Gesture Viewpoint in Japanese and English: Cross-Linguistic Interactions between Two Languages in One Speaker." *Gesture* 8 (2): 256–76.

Brown, A. L., J. D. Bransford, R. A. Ferrara, and J. C. Campione. 1983. "Learning, Remembering, and Understanding." In: J. H. Flavell and E. M. Markman (eds.), *Handbook of Child Psychology.* Vol. 3. NY: Wiley: 77–166

Burgess, Y., and S. Trinidad, S. 1997. "Young Children and Computers: Debating the Issues." *Australian Educational Computing* 12 (1): 16–21.

Candlin, C. 1987. In: R. Batstone. 1994. *Grammar.* Oxford: OUP.

Cassidy, S. 2004. "Learning Styles: An Overview of Theories, Models, and Measures." *Educational Psychology* 24: 419–44.

Cazden, C. 1983. "Adult Assistance to Language Development: Scaffolds, Models, and Direct Instruction." *Developing Literature.* Delaware: International Reading Association.

Celce-Murcia, M., ed. 1991. *Teaching English as a Second or Foreign Language.* 2nd ed. Boston: Heinle and Heinle.

Chamot, A. U., and J. M. O'Malley. 1994. *The CALLA Handbook: Implementing the Cognitive Academic Language Learning Approach.* Reading, MA: Addison-Wesley.

Chapman, D. W., and C.W. Snyder, Jr. 2000. *Can High Stakes National Testing Improve Instruction? Reexamining Conventional Wisdom.* Elsevier Science Ltd.

"Chapter 74. Curriculum Alignments." *ELPS. English Language Proficiency Standards.* Education Service Center. Region 20 (ESC-20). 25 Dec. 2007. 2 Jan. 2014. <http://portal.esc20.net/portal/page/portal/esc20public/ELPS_EnglishLanguageProficiencyStandards>

Collier, V. P. 1989. "How Long? A Synthesis of Research on Academic Achievement in Second Language." *TESOL Quarterly* 23: 509–31.

Collier, V. P. 1992. "A Synthesis of Studies Examining Long-Term Language Minority Student Data on Academic Achievement." *Bilingual Research Journal* 16 (1–2): 187–212.

Collier, V. P. 1995. "Acquiring a Second Language for School." *Directions in Language & Education* 1 (4): 1–10.

Collier, V. P. 1998. *Promoting Academic Success for ESL Students.* New Jersey Teachers of English to Speakers of Other Languages: Bilingual Educators.

Cooperstein, S., and E. Kocevar-Weidinger. 2004. "Beyond Active Learning: A Constructivist Approach to Learning." Reference Services Rev. 82.2: 141–48.

Crandall, J. 1992. "Content-Centered Instruction in the United States." *Annual Review of Applied Linguistics* 13: 111–26.

Crandall, J., J. Jaramillo, J. Olsen et al. 2002. "Using Cognitive Strategies to Develop English Language and Literature." Washington, DC: ERIC Clearinghouse on Languages and Linguistics, Center for Applied Linguistics.

Cummins, J. 1981. *Bilingualism and Minority Language Children.* Toronto: Institute for Studies in Education.

Cummins, J. 1984. *Bilingualism and Special Education: Issues in Assessment and Pedagogy.* San Diego: College Hill Press.

Cummins, J. 1998. "Rossell and Baker: Their Case for the Effectiveness of Bilingual Education." *Journal of Pedagogy Pluralism and Practice* 3 (1), Fall.

Cummins, J., and M. Genzuk. 1991. "Analysis of Final Report Longitudinal Study of Structured English Immersion Strategy, Early-Exit and Late-Exit Transitional Bilingual Education Programs for Language-minority Students." *California Association for Bilingual Education Newsletter* 13.

Day, R. R., and J. Bamford. 1998. *Extensive Reading in the Second Language Classroom.* Cambridge: CUP.

Díaz-Rico, L. T. 2008. *Strategies for Teaching English Learners.* 2nd ed. Boston: Pearson.

Díaz-Rico, L. T., and K. Z. Weed. 1995/2013. *Cross-Cultural, Language, and Academic Development Handbook: A Complete K-12 Reference Guide.* 5th ed., 2013. Needham Heights, MA: Allyn and Bacon.

Dulay, H., and M. Burt. 1974. "You Can't Learn without Goofing." In: J. Richards (ed.), *Error Analysis: Perspectives on Second Language Acquisition.* NY: Longman.

Echevarria, J. 1995. "Interactive Reading Instruction: A Comparison of Proximal and

Distal Effects of Instructional Conversations." *Exceptional Children* 61 (6): 536–52.

Ellis, R. 1994. *The Study of Second Language Acquisition.* Oxford: OUP.

ELPS: English Language Proficiency Standards. Education Service Center, Region 4 (ESC4), 2009. 2 Jan. 2014. <www.esc4.net/docs/122-ELPS.pdf>

Enright, D. S. 1991. "Supporting Children's English Language Development in Grade Level and Language Classrooms." (In: Celce-Murcia, M. 1991.)

Garcia, E. 2001. *Student Cultural Diversity: Understanding and Meeting the Challenge.* 3rd ed. Boston: Houghton Mifflin.

Gardner, H. *Intelligence Reframed: Multiple Intelligences for the 21st Century.* NY: Basic Books, 1999.

Gardner, R., and W. Lambert. 1972. *Attitudes and Motivation in Second Language Learning.* Cambridge, MA: Newbury House.

Genesee, F. 1987. *Learning through Two Languages: Studies of Immersion and Bilingual Education.* Cambridge, MA: Newbury House.

Genesee, F., ed. 1994. *Educating Second Language Children: The Whole Child, the Whole Curriculum, the Whole Community.* Cambridge: CUP.

Genesee, F., et al. 2006. *Conclusions and Future Directions.* NY: Cambridge University Press.

Goodman, K. S. 1986. *What's Whole about Whole Language? A Parent/Teacher Guide to Children's Learning.* Portsmouth, NH: Heinemann.

Grellet, F. 1981. *Developing Reading Skills.* Cambridge: CUP.

Graves, M., et al. 2012. *Teaching Vocabulary to English Languages Learners.* NY: Teachers College Press.

Hartley, K., and L. D. Bendixen. 2001. "Educational Research in the Internet Age: Examining the Role of Individual Characteristics." *Educational Researcher* 30 (9).

Hoven, D. 1992. "CALL in a Language Learning Environment." *CAELL Journal* 3 (2): 19–27.

Hoven, D. 1996. "Communicating and Interacting: An Exploration of the Changing Roles of Media in CALL/CMC." *Calico Journal* 23 (2): 233–56.

Hughes, A. 1989. *Testing for Language Teachers.* NY: CUP.

Johns, K. M., and N. M. Tórrez. "Helping ESL Learners Succeed." *Phi Delta Kappa* 484: 7–49.

Kramsch, C. 1998. *Language and Culture.* Oxford: OUP.

Krashen, S. 1982. *Principles and Practice in Second Language Acquisition.* Oxford: Pergamon Press.

Krashen, S., and T. Terrell. 1983. *The Natural Approach: Language Acquisition in the Classroom.* Oxford: Pergamon Press.

Larsen-Freeman, D. 1997. "Chaos/Complexity Science and Second Language Acquisition." *Applied Linguistics* 18 (2): 141–65.

McDonough, J., and S. Shaw. 1993. *Materials and Methods in ELT: A Teacher's Guide.* London: Blackwell.

McKeon, D. 1987. *Different Types of ESL Programs.* Washington, DC: ERIC Clearinghouse on Language and Linguistics.

McLaughlin, B. 1990. "The Development of Bilingualism: Myth and Reality." In: A. Barona and E. Garcia (eds.), *Children at Risk: Poverty, Minority Status, and Other Issues in Educational Equity.* Washington, DC: National Association of School Psychologists: 65–76.

Mohan, B., and W.-A. Lo. 1985. "Academic Writing and Chinese Students' Transfer and Developmental Factors." *TESOL Quarterly* 19: 515–34.

Moll, L. C. 1998. "Turning to the World: Bilingualism, Literacy and the Cultural Mediation of Thinking." *National Reading Conference Yearbook* 47: 59–75.

Murray, G., and S. Kouritzen. 1997. "Re-thinking Second Language Instruction, Autonomy and Technology: A Manifesto." *System* 25 (2): 185–96.

Ninio, A., and J. Bruner. 1988. "The Achievements and Antecedents of Labelling." In: M. Franklin and S. Barten (eds.), *Child Language: A Reader.* New York: Oxford University Press.

Nunan, D. 1989. *Designing Tasks for the Communicative Classroom.* Cambridge: CUP.

Padrón, Y. N., and H. C. Waxman. 1996. "Improving the Teaching and Learning of English Language Learners through Instructional Technology." *International Journal of Instructional Media,* 23 (4): 341–54.

Paris, S.G., and B. K. Lindauer. 1976. "The Role of Inference in Children's Comprehension and Memory." *Cognitive Psychology* 8: 217–27.

Peregoy, S. F., and O. F. Boyle. 2008. *Reading, Writing, and Learning in ESL.* 5th ed. Boston: Pearson.

Perera, K. 1993. "Standard English in Attainment of Target One." *Language Matters.* Centre for Primary Education 3: 10.

Prabhu, N. S. 1987. *Second Language Pedagogy: A Perspective.* London: Oxford: OUP.

Pressley, M. 2002. "What Should Reading Comprehension Instruction Be the Instruction of?" In M. Kamil, P. Mosenthal, P. D. Pearson, and R. Barr (eds.), *Handbook of Reading Research.* Vol. 3. Mahwah, NJ: Erlbaum: 545–61.

"Proficiency Level Descriptors." *Telpas Resources.* Texas Education Agency. 19 Dec. 2013. 2 Jan. 2014. <http://www.tea.state.tx.us/student.assessment/ell/telpas/>

Reid, J. "The Learning Style Preferences of ESL Students." *TESOL Quarterly,* 21(1): 86–103.

Reilly, T. 1998. "ESL through Content Area Instruction." ERIC No. ED296572. May 1988. 12 Feb. 2014. http://www.eric.ed.gov.

Rennie, J. 1993. "ESL and Bilingual Program Models." *Eric Digest.* Sept. 1993. 12 Feb. 2014. <http://www.cal.org/resources/Digest/rennie01.html>.

Reyhner, J. 1997. *Teaching Indigenous Languages.* Compilation of papers from a symposium at Northern Arizona University Department of Modern Languages. 25.2. Flagstaff, AZ.

Richards, Platt, and Weber. 1985. quoted by Ellis, R." The Evaluation of Communicative Tasks in Tomlinson, B (ed.)" *Materials Development in Language Teaching*. Cambridge: CUP. 1998.

Riding, R. J., and I. Cheema. 1991. "Cognitive Styles: An Overview and Integration." *Educational Psychology,* 11 (3, 4): 193–215.

Saunders, W. M., and C. Goldenberg. 1999. "Effects of Instructional Conversations and Literature Logs on Limited- and Fluent-English-Proficient Students' Story Comprehension and Thematic Understanding." *Elementary School Journal* 99 (4): 277–301.

Saville-Troike, M. 1986. "Anthropological Considerations in the Study of Communication," *Nature of Communication Disorders in Cuturally and Linguistically Diverse Populations.* San Diego: College Hill Press.

Schmidt, R., and S. Frota. 1986. "Developing Basic Conversational Ability in a Second Language: A Case Study of an Adult Learner in Portuguese." In: R. R. Day (ed.), *Talking to Learn: Conversation in Second Language Acquisition.* Rowley, MA: Newbury House: 237–326.

Schumm, J. S., ed. 2006. *Reading Assessment and Instruction for All Learners*. New York: Guilford Press.

Selinker, L. 1972. "Interlanguage." *International Review of Applied Linguistics in Language Teaching* 10 (3): 209.

Selinker, L. 1992. *Rediscovering Interlanguage.* London: Longman.

Sinclair, J., and M. Coulthard. 1975. *Towards an Analysis of Discourse.* Oxford: OUP: 93–94.

"State of Texas Assessments Comparison Chart." 2012. *STAAR® Resources.* Texas Education Agency. 17 Dec. 2013. 2 Jan. 2014. <http://www.tea.state.tx.us/student.assessment/staar/>

"Student Assessment in Texas." 2007–8. *Technical Digest,* Ch.1.

Teachers of English to Speakers of Other Languages. 1997. *ESL Standards for Pre–K-12 Students.* Alexandria, VA.: TESOL.

"TELPAS Resources." 2013. *Information on State Assessments for English Language Learners.* Texas Education Agency. 17 Dec. 2013. 2 Jan. 2014. <http://www.tea.state.tx.us/student.assessment/ell/>

"Texas Essential Knowledge and Skills for English Language Arts and Reading." 2011. *Texas Administrative Code.* Texas Education Agency. 22 Aug. 2011. 2 Jan. 2014. <http://ritter.tea.state.tx.us/rules/tac/chapter110/index.html>

"Texas State's Media Toolkit." *STAAR® Resources.* 2013. Texas Education Agency, 4 Nov. 2013. 2 Jan. 2014. <http://www.tea.state.tx.us/index2.aspx?id=2147504081>

Thomas, W. P., and V. P. Collier. 1995. *Language Minority Student Achievement and Program Effectiveness.* Manuscript in preparation. (In: Collier, V. P. 1995.)

Thompson, R. 1996. "Assimilation." *Encyclopedia of Social and Cultural Anthropology.* Vol. 1. NY: Henry Holt & Co: 11121–25.

Trudgill, P. 1984. *Applied Sociolinguistics.* University of Michigan: Academic Press.

Ur, P. 1996. *A Course in Language Teaching.* Cambridge: CUP.

Vygotsky, L. S. 1986. *Thought and Language.* Cambridge, MA: MIT Press.

Vygotsky, L. S. 2006. *Mind in Society*. Cambridge, MA: Harvard University Press.

Watson, S. 2011. Learning Disability Checklist. 12 Feb. 2014. <http://specialed.about.com/cs/learningdisabled/a/LDstrengthweak.htm >

Zainuddin, H., et al. 2007. *Fundamentals of Teaching English to Speakers of Other Languages in K-12 Mainstream Classrooms.* 2nd ed. Dubuque: Kendall/Hunt.

Zwiers, J. 2008. *Building Academic Language: Essential Practices for Content Classrooms, Grades 5–12.* San Francisco: Jossey-Bass.

Zwiers, J., and M. Crawford 2011. *Academic Conversations: Classroom Talk That Fosters Critical Thinking and Content Understandings.* Portland, ME: Stenhouse Publishers.

SAMPLE TEST 1

1. *Bite* and *byte* are examples of which phonographemic differences? (*Rigorous*) (*Skill* 1.1)

   A. Homonyms

   B. Homographs

   C. Homophones

   D. Heteronyms

2. **If you are studying** *syntax,* **then you are studying:** *(Easy) (Skill 1.1)*

   A. intonation and accent when conveying a message.

   B. the rules for correct sentence structure.

   C. the definition of individual words and meanings.

   D. the subject-verb-object order of the English sentence.

3. **Which one of the following is NOT a factor in people changing their register?** *(Rigorous) (Skill 1.2)*

   A. Relationship between the speakers

   B. Formality of the situation

   C. Attitude toward the listeners and the subject

   D. Culture of the speakers

4. **Culture and cultural differences:** *(Average) (Skill 1.3)*

   A. must be addressed by the teacher in the ELL classroom by pointing out cultural similarities and differences.

   B. should be the starting point for learning about how culture affects the ELL's attitude toward education.

   C. positively affects how well ELLs perform in the language classroom.

   D. may have strong emotional influence on the ELL.

5. **When referring to discourse in the English language, which is the most important principle for successful oral communication?** *(Easy) (Skill 1.4)*

   A. Taking "turns" in conversation

   B. Choice of topic

   C. The setting or context of the conversation

   D. Empty language

6. Polite discourse includes phrases such as "How are you?" or "See you later" as examples of:
(Easy) (Skill 1.4)

A. CALPs.

B. a skit.

C. empty language.

D. formal speech.

7. The affective domain affects how students acquire a second language because:
(Rigorous) (Skills 2.1, 6.4)

A. learning a second language may make the learner feel vulnerable.

B. the attitude of peers and family is motivating.

C. motivation is a powerful personal factor.

D. facilitative anxiety determines our reaction to competition and is positive.

8. Which of the following researchers theorized on the importance of repeating certain items in the language acquisition process?
(Rigorous) (Skill 2.2)

A. Cummins

B. Bialystok

C. Dulay and Burt

D. Vygotsky

9. The primary purpose of these questions is to help students:

A. use several cognitive strategies to internalize the new vocabulary.

B. develop strategies to correct misunderstandings.

C. become proficient at understanding their own language proficiency.

D. offset gaps in their current language abilities.

10. An example of simplification is:
(Easy) (Skill 2.4)

A. adding "ed" to irregular verbs as a way to use the past tense.

B. stating "I have a house beautiful in Miami" for "I have a beautiful house in Miami."

C. Hispanics pronouncing words that begin with "s" like "student" as "estudent."

D. asking someone "You like?" instead of "Do you like this one?"

11. Interlanguage is best described as:
(Easy) (Skill 2.5)

A. a language characterized by overgeneralization.

B. bilingualism.

C. a language-learning strategy.

D. a strategy characterized by poor grammar.

12. Vygotsky's zones of proximal development include activities that are:
(Average) (Skill 3.1)

A. adapted to students' current language capabilities.

B. used to teach the classroom goals.

C. related to prior knowledge.

D. culturally explicit.

13. Incorporating prior knowledge into L2 learning does NOT:
(Easy) (Skill 3.2)

A. permit readers to learn and remember more.

B. cause poor readers.

C. help readers to evaluate new arguments.

D. improve comprehension.

14. Which of the following is the best option for introducing new vocabulary to preliterate ELLs?
(Average) (Skill 3.2)

A. Wall charts

B. Word ladders

C. Stories

D. Spelling lists

15. If the teacher circulates around the room, answering questions and asking others, she is demonstrating which level(s) of scaffolding?
(Rigorous) (Skill 3.2)

A. Modeling

B. Interactive

C. Guided

D. Independent

16. **Which of the following activities would NOT be considered a communicative activity?**
(Easy) (Skill 3.3)

A. Problem-solving conversations

B. Debates

C. Teacher/student/teacher questions and answers

D. Peer interviews

17. **Which one of the following is NOT a reason for interactive group work?**
(Easy) (Skill 3.3)

A. Anxiety is lowered.

B. Materials are simplified.

C. Different thinking skills and oral skills can be utilized.

D. Social skills are developed.

18. **When using instructional technology (e.g., videos, DVDs, or CDs) in ESOL classes, the instructor should:**
(Rigorous) (Skill 3.4)

A. play the entire piece to build listening skills.

B. frequently stop to check on comprehension.

C. quiz the ELLs for comprehension after listening.

D. block the captions on the video.

DIRECTIONS: Use the information below to answer the questions that follow.

Ms. Rojas' second grade ESL class rotates through independent learning centers that support the week's reading objectives. One of the centers incorporates using a district's purchased reading software program to help students develop comprehension skills. Another center has eBooks available on the school's eReaders that address this week's topic. The third center has an art activity that incorporates one of the stories read as a class, and the fourth center has students sequencing the same story using pictures and simple sentences.

19. **Based on the information in this scenario, Ms. Rojas knows how to:**
(Average) (Skill 3.4)

A. apply knowledge of effective practices to engage students in critical thinking and grow their communication abilities.

B. select instructional methods, resources, and materials to address instructional goals for her ESL students.

C. design and implement instruction that fulfills the domains of listening, speaking, reading and writing.

D. integrate technology as a tool and resource to facilitate and enhance student learning.

20. After monitoring her students at the various centers, Ms. Rojas realizes that her students are struggling to read the sequence strips in the fourth center. Based on Ms. Rojas' observation, which of the following is the most appropriate support to add?
(Rigorous) (Skill 5.4)

A. Skimming to determine the main idea of each sentence and its proper placement in the story's sequence.

B. Key vocabulary word cards from each sentence with simple definitions that are read before beginning the activity.

C. Having students reread the story with a partner before beginning the activity.

D. Verbally summarizing the story as a group, discussing the various aspects of the story, such as problem/solution, character traits, and so on.

21. To better manage the movement between centers and student behavior during centers, which would be the best strategies for Ms. Rojas to use?
(Rigorous) (Skill 3.5)

A. Physically role-play expected work and behavior at each center and movement from one to the other.

B. Have each center identified with visual signs that students understand, such as geometric shapes and colors.

C. After practicing centers for one week, assign teams of students with similar abilities to rotate through centers.

D. Assign a team leader for each group to monitor behavior and collect the work that is being done.

22. Which activity could be used to explore the cultural heritage of many diverse countries?
(Average) (Skill 3.5)

A. Singing *Hava Nagila*

B. Composing original parodies (e.g., *On Top of Spaghetti*)

C. Comparing proverbs from different countries

D. Writing Haiku

23. Advanced TPR might include:
(Average) (Skill 4.1)

A. rapid-fire commands.

B. more advanced vocabulary.

C. funny commands.

D. All of the above

24. Communication involves specific skills such as:
(Average) (Skill 4.2)

A. turn-taking.

B. silent period.

C. lexical chunks.

D. repetition.

25. The fifth grade content-area teacher has decided to use stories in her classroom for all students. What would be the best strategy to use so that ELLs also participate? *(Rigorous) (Skill 4.3)*

    A. Discuss favorite stories with the class

    B. Bring in picture books of children's stories

    C. Have children draw their own story

    D. Group students together and have them retell their favorite movie

26. Which of the following activities would encourage authentic oral language production in ELLs? *(Average) (Skill 4.4)*

    A. Group work

    B. Oral quizzes

    C. One-on-one interview with teacher

    D. Oral reports

27. Which of the following activities is probably the most meaningful for developing ELLs' communicative skills? *(Rigorous) (Skill 4.4)*

    A. Cloze procedure activities

    B. Gap-filling activities

    C. Role plays and skits

    D. TPR

28. Which of the following options is best for the ESOL teacher to use to activate background knowledge? *(Average) (Skill 4.4)*

    A. Demonstration using realia

    B. Asking questions about the topic using a picture to illustrate it

    C. Reading the text with the ELL and explaining "as you go"

    D. Allowing the ELL to watch a video on the school intranet

29. Ms. Torres has completed testing her new ESL student in his native language of Spanish for reading and finds that he does not have a strong phonological awareness of the language. She then enlists the help of the grade-level bilingual teacher to include the new student in the after-school tutoring in Spanish reading. What is the reason that Ms. Torres does this? *(Rigorous) (Skill 4.5)*

    A. She is aware that the student is unable to identify cognates in both Spanish and English.

    B. She recognizes the importance of the student transferring skills in the first language to the second language.

    C. She knows that the success of the student is directly connected to recognizing subject-verb agreement in the second language.

    D. She recognizes that working in the student's native language will help him feel more comfortable.

30. Which of the following options is probably the most beneficial to ELLs who do not yet read in their native language?
(Easy) (Skill 4.6)

A. Instruction based on needs

B. Involving the ELL's family

C. Oral storytelling in the classroom

D. Using the same methods of instruction as used for native speakers

31. Which of the following options is the best nonintrusive way to make a correction?
(Easy) (Skill 4.7)

A. Suggesting a better or additional alternative

B. Having the ELL who made the error write the correction

C. Asking the ELL's peers to correct the error

D. Repeating the errors on an error sheet and asking students to correct them

DIRECTIONS: Use the information below to answer the questions that follow.

Mr. Richards is planning to assess his twelfth grade students in his biology class over the sequence of steps needed to conduct an experiment. He knew that several of his ELLs struggle to understand simple concept discussions and are hesitant to seek clarification, often remaining silent and watching their lab partners for clues. Yet his anecdotal records of these students show that their social language skills are improving although they still rely upon gestures, visuals, and are speaking slower than their peers. Based on these records, Mr. Richards decides to implement accommodations to support his ELLs before assessing them.

32. Based on Mr. Richards' observations, you may conclude that several of his ELLs are functioning as _____ in listening.
(Average) (Skill 5.1)

A. beginning ELLs

B. intermediate ELLs

C. advanced ELLs

D. advanced-high ELLs

33. After developing a series of accommodations for listening and reading for his ELLs, Mr. Richards began implementing those that would facilitate his students' acquisitions of the main concepts. Which of the following would NOT support his beginning-level ELLs' listening abilities?
(Average) (Skill 5.2)

A. Provide extended wait time for processing new information.

B. Explicitly teach note-taking strategies during discussions.

C. Use shorter, less complex sentences when giving information.

D. Use visuals to increase comprehension.

34. Despite the accommodations, the majority of Mr. Richards' ELLs did not pass the test. After talking with his students, Mr. Richards discovered they did not understand the directions or format of the test. Based on this information, the best strategy to use for the retest is for Mr. Richards to:
(Rigorous) (Skill 7.1)

A. provide future modified oral assessments.

B. use performance-based assessments for the remainder of the year.

C. encourage the use of bilingual glossaries or dictionaries.

D. chunk the directions into steps to be read aloud and modeled before the test.

35. Which of the following is NOT an appropriate instructional practice for beginning readers?
(Rigorous) (Skill 5.3)

A. Chunking of text

B. Modeled reading

C. Dictation of reading words

D. Word reading practice

36. Schema theory suggests that for learning to take place, teachers must:
(Average) (Skill 5.5)

A. integrate content areas with ESOL techniques.

B. emphasize all four language skills.

C. present comprehensible input in a meaningful context.

D. relate new materials to previous knowledge.

37. In a kindergarten classroom, the teacher designed a language experience story on plants after the children observed bean seeds sprouting and developing leaves. This activity followed good ESOL practice because:
(Average) (Skill 5.6)

A. background knowledge was activated.

B. plants were part of the science curriculum.

C. the story represented genuine communication.

D. All of the above

DIRECTIONS: Use the information below to answer the questions that follow.

Ms. Rollman noticed that Alicia is struggling in her ESL fourth grade self-contained classroom and is not acquiring English language reading skills as readily as her other ESL classmates. Alicia is unable to remember basic sight words and has difficulty writing simple sentences yet is able to communicate with her peers. When Ms. Rollman looked through Alicia's records, she noticed that Alicia only experiences English while at school. She also found that Alicia's parents denied the services of a bilingual classroom yet opted for an ESL placement, believing that a bilingual classroom would inhibit Alicia's education. Alicia's records also indicate that her first language placement test shows that she is at grade level in reading when using her first language yet is at a primary level in English. Based on this information, Ms. Rollman knows that she will have to alter her approach with Alicia and create bridges between her first and second language while also addressing her language development.

38. By accessing Alicia's folder and analyzing the data, Ms. Rollman shows that she:
(Rigorous) (Skill 5.7)

A. knows reading comprehension factors that can affect ESL students' reading comprehension and language development.

B. understands the strategies necessary to build Alicia's sight word recognition.

C. knows that the acquisition of English is developed over time through extensive practice in both speaking and listening.

D. realizes how Alicia's lack of exposure to English outside of the classroom is affecting her literacy development.

39. Based on her findings, Ms. Rollman begins to use a more cooperative learning environment for Alicia and her ESL students. She also incorporates more graphic organizers during content introduction and seeks to make more connections between Alicia's background knowledge and the content currently being studied through reading and speaking activities. By doing these activities, Ms. Rollman:
(Rigorous) (Skill 6.2)

A. is using a task-based or experiential learning classroom setting to ensure success of the ELLs.

B. shows that she understands which instructional delivery practices are effective in developing ELLs' comprehension.

C. realizes that a whole-language approach is the best delivery of content for ELLs' comprehension.

D. shows that she realizes the importance of silent, sustained reading opportunities for content information and acquisition.

40. **Knowing that there was a wide disparity between Alicia's reading comprehension in her native language in comparison to her second language, the best approach for Ms. Rollman would be to:**
(Rigorous) (Skill 1.3)

    A. focus on developing Alicia's phonological awareness of both her native language and the target language.

    B. encourage more academic discourse through listening and speaking.

    C. use more guided discussions in the content areas currently being studied.

    D. use more sight word recognition strategies to enhance Alicia's fluency.

41. **Based on Alicia's data, Ms. Rollman researched the types of ESL programs offered at her school. Ms. Rollman spoke with Alicia's parents, who agreed to let Alicia take part in a bilingual class during part of the school day. Which of the following types of ESL programs would be the best fit for Alicia?**
(Average) (Skill 8.2)

    A. Structured English immersion

    B. English as a Second Language pull-out program

    C. Submersion with primary language support

    D. Self-contained

DIRECTIONS: Use the information below to answer the questions that follow.

Mr. Solis' fourth grade class is working on understanding the theory of plate tectonics in Science. Due to the large amount of vocabulary to be learned and the level of difficulty, Mr. Solis places students in groups, gives them the assigned reading, a graphic organizer for information, and a simplified rubric for students to follow. Mr. Solis' needs to know if students are able to transfer information from a graphic organizer to an essay, so he plans to have students create a short, diagnostic essay on the theory of plate tectonics. As students are working in groups, Mr. Solis takes anecdotal records on individuals, noting difficulties and achievements.

42. **Based on this information, Mr. Solis obviously understand the importance of:**
(Average) (Skill 6.1)

    A. peer-mediated instruction.

    B. Socratic dialogue.

    C. peer tutoring.

    D. whole-language implementation.

43. **Based on the information in the scenario, Mr. Solis knows that having students write an essay is an excellent way to diagnose:** *(Rigorous) (Skill 7.1)*

   A. students' proficiency in the target language and vocabulary of the content

   B. students' strengths and weaknesses in the targeted objective

   C. one student against another in acquisition of skills

   D. students' acquired skills before testing

DIRECTIONS: Use the information below to answer the questions that follow.

Mr. Alvera teaches a third grade self-contained ESL class. Every nine weeks the district conducts a district-wide assessment on reading, writing, and science. Mr. Alvera is keeping track of the progress his ELLs are making based on their assessment scores. On Friday, Mr. Alvera meets with his students to discuss their thinking processes for solving particular problems as well as their assessment results. They work together to plan what objectives need to be reviewed and retaught during the following week.

44. **It is obvious that Mr. Alvera:** *(Rigorous) (Skill 7.6)*

   A. knows basic concepts, issues, and practices related to test design and uses this knowledge to select and develop assessments.

   B. knows how to use ongoing assessments to plan and adjust instruction that addresses individual student needs, enabling students to achieve learning goals.

   C. applies knowledge of formal and informal assessments used in the ESL classroom and understands their uses.

   D. knows standardized tests used in the ESL program in the state of Texas and how to interpret them.

45. **Mr. Alvera understands how to further his students' mastery of content-area learning by using which of the following strategies?** *(Average) (Skill 6.2)*

   A. The use of metacognition with students to help them recognize their thinking processes

   B. The use of sequenced and scaffold assessments to formulate future instruction

   C. The development of ESL instruction that is linguistically accommodated to the students' level of English

   D. The importance of using critical thinking to aid in the development of students' academic-language proficiency

DIRECTIONS: Use the information below to answer the questions that follow.

Ms. Trinidad received a new ELL with little English whose parents have refused bilingual services. In reviewing his academic record, and using personal anecdotal records, Ms. Trinidad quickly recognizes that he has a well-grounded understanding of mathematics but lacks the content-area vocabulary in English. Knowing that this directly affects his learning, Ms. Trinidad begins to implement strategies for addressing this problem.

46. **Based on this information, Ms. Trinidad realizes the importance of which of the following?** *(Rigorous) (Skill 6.4)*

    A. Effective resources

    B. Instructional delivery practices that are effective in helping ELLs

    C. The personal factors that affect ELLs' content-area learning

    D. The individual differences in cultural backgrounds

47. **Based on the information in the scenario, which of the following would be the best practices and resources for Ms. Trinidad to use?** *(Rigorous) (Skill 6.2)*

    A. Providing written vocabulary words and phrases that are applicable to the content

    B. Creating critical thinking intervention while developing academic language proficiency in the content

    C. Recognizing language background and learning styles to develop strategies for learning the content

    D. Preteaching content vocabulary and helping the student apply familiar concepts to new learning experiences

48. Ms. Bueno's fifth grade ELL mathematics class is working on developing problem-solving strategies to solve word problems. Knowing that there are several individuals who need a visual representation of the problem's language, she introduces the strategy of drawing a picture to solve a problem. By having her students individually draw a picture to represent the problem, Ms. Bueno shows that she understands the importance of which of the following? (Rigorous) (Skill 6.3)

A. Building upon prior knowledge to identify vocabulary

B. Developing students' cognitive processes

C. The use of cooperative learning in the classroom

D. Providing experiential learning opportunities

DIRECTIONS: Use the information below to answer the questions that follow.

The physical education teacher in a Texas elementary school combines two bilingual classes with one ESL class. Knowing that the majority of the students are not fluent in English, the P.E. teacher creates an activity to accommodate their level of language acquisition. Creating posters to visually show students what to do for each section of the dance, students will demonstrate the main objective of the activity by dancing the complete sequence of steps as an assessment.

However, the teacher noticed there was confusion and a lack of ability to do the complete routine. After meeting with the other teachers and analyzing students' language placement, the P.E. teacher decided to alter the activity to ensure that all students would be successful and willing to participate in the assessment.

49. In order to understand each child's language level, the P.E. teacher would best refer to the results of which assessment? (Average) (Skill 7.2)

A. TELPAS

B. AAPPL

C. TOEFL

D. STAAR

50. Which of the following would be the best alteration to the activity if the goal is that all students participate in the final assessment? (Rigorous) (Skill 8.4)

A. The posters are rewritten in the first language of the majority of the students with visual images to show what is expected.

B. As a class, students say and mimic the words and actions of the P.E. teacher through each stage of the dance.

C. Students are placed into groups of four instead of six, and are given more time at each station.

D. The P.E. teacher brings in a bilingual aide to explain the stations and the final product of a dance to the whole group.

51. Before coming to the U.S., Sven, an eleventh grade student, took the TOEFL. This is a _____ test. *(Easy) (Skill 7.2)*

A. language proficiency

B. language achievement

C. language placement

D. diagnostic language

52. An eighth grade ESL teacher is struggling to understand why her ELLs are doing poorly in her literature class. After reviewing their STAAR scores from the previous year, the teacher realizes that these students have done poorly in the past year in reading comprehension. If the teacher wants more information of their growth in reading English, which of the following would be the best course of action to take? *(Rigorous) (Skill 7.3)*

A. Using a district assessment in each student's native language.

B. Reassessing students with a STAAR-released test.

C. Reviewing students' proficiency levels from previous TELPAS exams.

D. Meeting with the LPAC to review students' placement in the ESL program.

DIRECTIONS: Use the information below to answer the questions that follow.

Julio, an eighth grade ELL, wrote the following paragraph in his American history class.

A govenor is some one who runs a state. In the u s. It can be a man or women. A govenor is elected. By the people of the state. The man or women can be a govenor. The govenor makes laws.

53. Which of the following English-language proficiency levels best describes Julio's writing? *(Average) (Skill 7.3)*

A. Beginning

B. Intermediate

C. Advanced

D. Advanced high

54. Julio's American history teacher shared his writing with the language arts teacher. Based on what the language arts teacher sees in the writing sample, the best accommodations that the history teacher could use would be which of the following?
(Rigorous) (Skill 5.2)

A. Focus on compound and complex sentences and using mini-lessons on grammatical structures within a complex sentence.

B. Focus on the use of graphic organizers with extensive time to work through the writing process with mini-lessons on the use of transitions and prepositions.

C. Focus on simple and compound sentence structure using graphic organizers for writing organization with mini-lessons focusing on grammar usage.

D. Focus on the use of bilingual dictionaries and content-area glossaries while using mini-lessons that focus on grammatical structures.

55. Mr. Garcia, a high school algebra teacher, notices within the first few weeks of school that Jasmine is struggling in class. While she is able to do the actual computation when it comes to analyzing word problems, Jasmine struggles to comprehend their meaning. Mr. Garcia knows that Jasmine was exited from the ESL program so he meets with the school's LPAC to discuss his concerns. At the conclusion of the meeting, the committee agrees to follow established state guidelines to help Jasmine. Which of the following is the best objective to follow, based on state guidelines?
(Average) (Skill 7.4)

A. Mr. Garcia will arrange a meeting with Jasmine's parents.

B. Jasmine will be placed back in an ESL class until graduation.

C. Jasmine will be take an oral language assessment in her native language.

D. Jasmine's academic progress will be monitored for the next two years.

56. Which of the following is NOT an acceptable alternative assessment strategy for ELLs?
(Average) (Skill 7.5)

A. Portfolios

B. Observation

C. Self-assessment

D. Essay writing

57. In *Lau* v. *Nichols* (1974), the Supreme Court ruled that: (Rigorous) (Skill 8.1)

A. school districts may not continue education programs that fail to produce positive results for ELLs.

B. sexual harassment in any school activity on or off campus is prohibited.

C. students were denied an "equal" education.

D. discrimination against students and employees based on race, ethnicity, national origins, disability, or marital status is prohibited.

58. The No Child Left Behind Act established that: (Rigorous) (Skill 8.1)

A. Title I funds are available only if the schools participate in the National Assessment of Education Progress.

B. bilingual programs must be effective and meet three established criteria.

C. high-performing children cannot be used to average out low-performing ELLs.

D. schools must form and convene assessment committees.

59. Bilingualism of ELLs can be greatly improved by: (Average) (Skill 8.2)

A. a block schedule.

B. the community's value of the L2.

C. speaking L2 in the school.

D. interference occurring between L1 and L2.

60. Experts on bilingualism recommend: (Average) (Skill 8.2)

A. the use of the native language (mother tongue) until schooling begins.

B. reading in L1 while speaking L2 in the home.

C. exposing the child to both languages as early as possible.

D. speaking the language of the school as much as possible.

61. **When a school district implements a pull-out program model for their ELL population, there are a variety of material factors that they need to consider. Which of the following would be the best factor to consider?**
(Average) (Skill 8.3)

    A. State-adopted reading materials for the regular classroom

    B. Available classrooms

    C. Availability of manipulatives

    D. Diversity of leveled reading materials

62. **Which of the following options is NOT appropriate to content-based instruction (CBI)?**
(Average) (Skill 8.4)

    A. Asking silly questions

    B. Speaking at a normal pace

    C. Using visual cues

    D. Restating errors

63. **An ELL who has been living in the United States for many years is making little progress in her ESL class. Her family and friends live in the same neighborhood as many of her relatives from her native land. Which of the following conditions would probably have the most positive effect on the student's English language development?**
(Rigorous) (Skill 9.1)

    A. Reducing the time spent listening to and viewing media in the native language

    B. Decreasing the use of the native language in the home

    C. Adopting external elements of U.S. culture such as music and clothing

    D. Increasing social contact with members of U.S. culture

64. **Which of the following would be the best way to create a culturally responsive learning environment for ELLs in the classroom?**
(Average) (Skills 9.2, 9.3)

    A. Placing new students in the center or front of the classroom

    B. Providing parents with classroom information in their native language

    C. Having a range of materials, including educational technology

    D. Celebrating appropriate cultural holidays and celebrations

65. Amelia is conscientious in her studies, but she can't seem to finish and gets angry when the teacher tells her to hand in her paper. Which of the following cultural elements most likely explains the situation? *(Easy) (Skill 9.4)*

   A. Family structure

   B. Roles and interpersonal relationships

   C. Discipline

   D. Time

66. A high school ESL teacher with a class in careers and vocational studies has several subscriptions to newspapers, career magazines, and Internet cultural centers for the surrounding area. The teacher helps students isolate information from multinational organizations and identify career opportunities in which having a second language is essential for volunteer participation or application for a job. By using these materials, the ESL teacher is helping students: *(Average) (Skill 9.5)*

   A. determine what they want to focus on for careers in their area.

   B. realize the benefits and needs of being bilingual in the current workforce.

   C. understand the varieties of cultural organizations available to the population.

   D. determine the bilingual benefits of colleges and local community colleges.

67. **A newly immigrated family has expressed the desire to mingle with native-speaking Americans in order to polish their English-speaking skills. Which one of the following actions would probably be the most appropriate and effective in addressing the mother's and father's needs to mingle with native-speaking Americans?**
(Easy) (Skill 10.1)

   A. Suggest a private class in their home

   B. Provide literature about the programs for diet and exercise, offered at the local mall

   C. Mention the YMCA/YWCA and their services

   D. Recommend the public library and its adult programs

68. **Eighty-six percent of the students enrolled at a local elementary school are considered bilingual or ELL with Spanish being the predominant language. While planning a Science Night for students and parents, the ESL lead teacher talks with the PTO's Spanish-speaking members who volunteer to help families at the various stations during the event. Doing so shows that the ESL lead teacher:**
(Average) (Skill 10.2)

   A. knows how important it is to encourage participation of Spanish-speaking families in the school's activities.

   B. is advocating for the school's ELLs during the Science Night activities.

   C. knows how community resources can affect student learning.

   D. knows that there might not be enough adult participation in the Science Night activities.

69. The school is planning a Grandparents Day. Which of the following activities could be best used to promote the ESOL program?
(Easy) (Skill 10.3)

A. A bake sale

B. Sports activities (e.g., yoga, soccer, etc.)

C. Skits by children

D. Simple board games incorporating ESOL techniques

70. Which one of the following points is the aim of the 2009 version of the DREAM Act?
(Average) (Skill 10.4)

A. Promote military service or college education of older undocumented immigrants

B. Permit children who immigrated to the U.S. at an early age to acquire legal status independently of their parents

C. Encourage good moral character from illicit immigrants

D. Advocate education for legal aliens

SAMPLE TEST 1 ANSWER KEY AND RIGOR TABLE

Sample Test 1 Answer Key

1. C	11. C	21. A	31. A	41. C	51. A	61. B
2. B	12. A	22. C	32. A	42. A	52. C	62. B
3. D	13. B	23. D	33. B	43. B	53. B	63. D
4. D	14. C	24. A	34. D	44. B	54. C	64. A
5. A	15. B	25. D	35. C	45. A	55. D	65. D
6. C	16. C	26. A	36. D	46. C	56. D	66. B
7. A	17. B	27. C	37. D	47. D	57. C	67. D
8. C	18. B	28. A	38. D	48. B	58. C	68. A
9. A	19. D	29. B	39. B	49. A	59. B	69. D
10. D	20. B	30. A	40. A	50. B	60. C	70. B

Sample Test 1 Rigor Table

Rigor Level	Questions
Easy (20%)	2, 5, 6, 10, 11, 13, 16, 17, 30, 31, 51, 65, 67, 69
Average (40%)	4, 12, 14, 19, 22, 23, 24, 26, 28, 32, 33, 36, 37, 41, 42, 45, 49, 53, 55, 56, 59, 60, 61, 62, 64, 66, 68, 70
Rigorous (40%)	1, 3, 7, 8, 9, 15, 18, 20, 21, 25, 27, 29, 34, 35, 38, 39, 40, 43, 44, 46, 47, 48, 57, 50, 52, 54, 58, 63

SAMPLE TEST 1 ANSWERS WITH RATIONALES

1. **Answer: C. Homophones**
   (*Rigorous*) (*Skill* 1.1)
   Homonyms is a general term for a group of words that are spelled and sound alike or words that are spelled the same, but have two or more meanings. *Homographs* are two or more words with the same spelling or pronunciation, but they have different meanings. *Heteronyms* are two or more words that have the same spelling, but different meanings and spellings. *Homophones* are words that, like *bite* and *byte*, have the same pronunciation but different meanings and spellings.

2. **Answer: B. the rules for correct sentence structure**
   (*Easy*) (*Skill* 1.1)
   The intonation and accent used when conveying a message refer to pitch and stress. The definition of individual words and meanings is semantics. The subject-verb-object order of the English sentence refers to the correct order for most English sentences, but the rules for correct sentence structure refers to syntax, so B is the best option.

3. **Answer: D. Culture of the speakers**
   (*Rigorous*) (*Skill* 1.2)
   People change their register depending on the relationship between the speakers, the formality of the situation, and the attitudes toward the listeners and the subject. Option D, culture of the speakers, is not a reason for people to change their register.

4. **Answer: D. may have strong emotional influence on the ELL**
   (*Average*) (*Skill* 1.3)
   Culture and cultural differences may be addressed by the skillful ESOL teacher, but frequently teachers are unaware of all the cultures and cultural differences they are dealing with. At the same time, it may be possible to determine how his or her culture affects the ELL's attitude toward education; however, it may well be something the young child cannot express, or the adult hides for various reasons. Culture and cultural differences do not always play a positive role in the learning process and may have a strong emotional influence on the ELL, whether it is negative or positive. Thus, D is our best option.

5. **Answer: A. Taking "turns" in conversation**
   (*Easy*) (*Skill* 1.4)
   For discourse to be successful in any language, a set of ingrained social rules and discourse patterns must be followed. The choice of topic and setting, or context, of the conversation are important elements of discourse in English, but not the most important ones. Empty language refers to perfunctory speech that has little meaning but is important in social exchanges. In oral English discourse, taking "turns" is primordial.

6. **Answer: C. empty language**
(Easy) (Skill 1.4)
The two statements are examples of empty language that is used in polite discourse, but carries very little meaning.

7. **Answer: A. learning a second language may make the learner feel vulnerable**
(Rigorous) (Skills 2.1, 6.4)
The affective domain refers to the full range of human feelings and emotions that come into play during second-language acquisition. Learning a second language may make the learner feel vulnerable because he or she may have to leave his or her comfort zone behind. This can be especially difficult for adults who are used to being "powerful" or "in control" in their profession, but it also affects children and teens.

8. **Answer: C. Dulay and Burt**
(Rigorous) (Skill 2.2)
Dulay and Burt believed that the repetition of certain items in the target language contributed to the learner's output. Cummins focused on distinguishing between BICS and CALP. Bialystok theorized that the cognitive and academic development in the first language affects schooling in L2. Vygotsky studied the relationship between the development of thought and language.

9. **Answer: A. use several cognitive strategies to internalize the new vocabulary**
(Rigorous) (Skill 2.3)
Option A is correct because each question addresses a different strategy that students can use to help make connections to self, other text, media or the world, visualization, word patterns, and the use of flashcards for language proficiency. Options B, C, and D do not help students reflect upon their own use of strategies for problem-solving misunderstandings when communicating or reading.

10. **Answer: D. asking someone "You like?" instead of "Do you like this one?"**
(Easy) (Skill 2.4)
Simplification is a common learner error involving simplifying the language when the correct structures have not been internalized. In this case, the correct question form has not been acquired though the ELL's meaning is clear.

11. **Answer: C. a language-learning strategy**
(Easy) (Skill 2.5)
Interlanguage occurs when the second-language learner lacks proficiency in L2 and tries to compensate for his or her lack of fluency in the new language. Three components are overgeneralization, simplification, and L1 interference or language transfer. Therefore, Option A is only one component of interlanguage, making Option C the correct answer.

12. **Answer: A. adapted to students' current language capabilities**
(Average) (Skill 3.1)
Vygotsky's *zones of proximal development* refers to making students feel comfortable so that they are willing to take risks in their learning, especially in learning English. Activities should be adapted

to ELLs' current language and literacy or Vygotsky's zones of proximal development.

13. **Answer: B. cause poor readers**
(Easy) (Skill 3.2)
Activating schema and incorporating previous knowledge into L2 learning will strengthen the learning process. It certainly does not cause poor readers.

14. **Answer: C. Stories**
(Average) (Skill 3.2)
Wall charts and word ladders are excellent scaffolding devices for helping ELLs remember the words they are studying. Spelling lists help them remember specific words and how to spell them. Option C is the best option for introducing new words. Here the ELLs get the opportunity to see the words used in context and later learn the ones they don't already know.

15. **Answer: B. Interactive**
(Rigorous) (Skill 3.2)
If the teacher were modeling, she would be demonstrating correct pronunciation or syntax to the students. If the ELLs were at an independent level, they would not need scaffolding. By circulating and answering questions, she can be interactive—possibly through asking other questions.

16. **Answer: C. Teacher/student/ teacher questions and answers**
(Easy) (Skill 3.3)
In communicative activities, both parties gain meaningful insights into the topic at hand. Problem-solving conversations, debates, and peer interviews are examples.

Teacher/student/teacher questions and answers are not. They are ways in which the teacher controls the "communication" and learning activity—little is gained—or learned—by either party.

17. **Answer: B. Materials are simplified**
(Easy) (Skill 3.3)
Options A, B, and D are all valid reasons to engage students in pairs or small groups. Option B is correct because it is not a valid reason for interactive group work. Materials can be of different levels, even difficult levels to challenge more advanced students.

18. **Answer: B. frequently stop to check on comprehension**
(Rigorous) (Skill 3.4)
Option A would be tiring and boring for most ELLs. Listening for long periods of time before they are ready causes most language learners to "tune out." Option C would raise the affective filter and lessen language learning. Option D omits a source of visual information for ELLs. Option B is correct, because the teacher can stop the video and check to see that everyone understands. This practice will maintain motivation and increase interest.

19. **Answer: D. integrate technology as a tool and resource to facilitate and enhance student learning**
(Average) (Skill 3.4)
Ms. Rojas is using technology to support the reading objectives for the week. The integration of technology into an instructional process facilitates and enhances students' learning. Option A is not correct as

the goal of the centers is not on communication but rather reading comprehension. Option B is incorrect as the materials and resources are for all students and no indication is given that it is geared toward her ELLs. Option C is not correct as the centers are only geared toward the domain of reading.

20. **Answer: B. Key vocabulary word cards from each sentence with simple definitions that are read before beginning the activity** *(Rigorous) (Skill 5.4)*
Vocabulary is a known factor that affects ESL students reading comprehension. Not knowing vocabulary that is being used can impede a student's comprehension. The activity in the fourth center requires students to read so identifying problem words and presenting them in context would be the best support to add. Option A is not correct because skimming requires understanding of the text. Option C is incorrect because students are using sentences that have been simplified from the original story. Option D is not correct as verbally summarizing and discussing various aspects of the story will not help them read the sentences given.

21. **Answer: A. Physically role-play expected work and behavior at each center and movement from one to the other** *(Rigorous) (Skill 3.5)*
Option A is the best choice of a strategy to implement to ensure the best classroom management during center activities. By physically modeling expectations, students can see, hear, and ask questions before beginning the activities. In Option B, just having a visual sign will not help students to understand movement between centers nor expected behavior in the center. Option C is not correct because classroom management expectations should be in place at the start of the school term. In Option D, assigning one student to oversee others will hinder that student's learning, and he or she should not be expected to monitor the behavior of others.

22. **Answer: C. Comparing proverbs from different countries** *(Average) (Skill 3.5)*
Options A, B, and D are country-specific. Option C provides the opportunity to compare proverbs from different countries. By demonstrating to ELLs and their classmates that many countries share similar sayings or proverbs on universal topics, teachers sponsor the idea of cultural unity.

23. **Answer: D. All of the above** *(Average) (Skill 4.1)*
Total Physical Response (TPR) can be done slowly as a beginning activity for ELLs. As they begin to understand more oral English and the game, TPR can be "spiced up" by all of the suggestions.

24. **Answer: A. turn-taking** *(Average) (Skill 4.2)*
The silent period refers to a preproduction period observed before the ELL begins communicating. Lexical chunks are blocks of language used in everyday speech and writing. Repetition is used as a clarification technique or a

stalling technique before the ELL is ready to proceed. All are part of the language-acquisition process. There are many skills involved in communication, but the only one listed is turn-taking.

25. Answer: D. Group students together and have them retell their favorite movie
(Rigorous) (Skill 4.3)
Grouping students lessens the pressure of performing for the entire class. By discussing a favorite movie, students are given the chance to use language as they would in a natural context. Even underprivileged ELLs have access to a TV and/or movies that they can relate to others using the language they know to talk about something they enjoyed.

26. Answer: A. Group work
(Average) (Skill 4.4)
Options B, C, and D can be stressful for any student but especially an ELL who is concerned about his or her language skills. However, group work permits ELLs to work with their peers toward a common goal and encourages the use of authentic language in a relaxed atmosphere.

27. Answer: C. Role plays and skits
(Rigorous) (Skill 4.4)
Options A and B are written activities and would not contribute to communicative competence. TPR is a listening exercise. Option C is the best option for developing the ability to communicate in a "spontaneous" manner.

28. Answer: A. Demonstration using realia
(Average) (Skill 4.4)
All the activities will activate background knowledge if done well and if appropriate materials are used. Even so, using authentic materials while seeing, touching, and visualizing real objects as they are being discussed or used in demonstrations is the best option for activating background knowledge.

29. Answer: B. She recognizes the importance of the student transferring skills in the first language to the second language.
(Rigorous) (Skill 4.5)
If ELLs are able to read in their native language, they can then transfer the skills from their first language to the new second language. In this case, the student needs to strengthen his phonological awareness. Options A and C are not correct because the identification of cognates and subject-verb agreement are developed after strengthening phonological awareness. Option D is incorrect as no evidence is given that the student feels uncomfortable.

30. Answer: A. Instruction based on needs
(Easy) (Skill 4.6)
ELLs who do not read in their native language may come from societies where storytelling or other oral traditions are used. They may not have had the privilege of going to school because of conflicts in the area where they lived, they worked to increase the family income, or they lived in a rural area where there were no schools. Their first school experience may be in the U.S., so instruction based upon each child's

specific needs will probably be the most successful option when dealing with this situation.

31. Answer: A. Suggesting a better or additional alternative
(Easy) (Skill 4.7)
Option A gives immediate feedback and is likely to be the most helpful approach. Options B, C, and D might embarrass the learner.

32. Answer: A. beginning ELLs
(Average) (Skill 5.1)
Beginning-level ELLs often fail to seek clarification in English when not comprehending what they hear, often remaining silent and watching others for cues. These students struggle to understand discussions, relying on others for cues and clues, as well as often remaining silent. By contrast, intermediate ELLs have the ability to seek clarification in English and often identify and distinguish key words and phrases necessary to understanding. Advanced ELLs understand main points, important details, and only occasionally require or request that information be repeated. Advanced-high ELLs rarely require or request that information be repeated or rephrased to clarify what is being said and often participate in classroom discussions.

33. Answer: B. Explicitly teach note-taking strategies during discussions
(Average) (Skill 5.2)
Students classified as beginning ELLs for listening do not have the ability to take notes during verbal presentations as they will have difficulty processing what they are

hearing. This is a strategy to be used with advanced-high ELLs. Option A is not correct because extended wait time is a key component in helping beginning ELLs process between their first language and the new one. Option C is incorrect because using shorter, less complex sentences helps the beginning ELL focus on listening to the content of the sentence. Option D is not correct because providing beginning ELLs with visual clues helps them make connections between what they know and what they hear.

34. Answer: D. chunk the directions into steps to be read aloud and modeled before the test
(Rigorous) (Skill 7.1)
Option D is the best strategy to use because this will enable students to better understand how to take the test and to understand its format. Options A, B, and C are not the best strategies as this would not expose students to either the directions or format of a multiple-choice test.

35. Answer: C. Dictation of reading words
(Rigorous) (Skill 5.3)
Options A, B, and D are types of instruction that improve fluency (there are others). Option C, however, is used to improve spelling and is, therefore, the correct answer.

36. Answer: D. relate new materials to previous knowledge
(Average) (Skill 5.5)
The schema theory suggests that schemas need to be activated to draw upon the prior knowledge and learning of the ELL, especially when the ELL may not have had similar

experiences to learners in mainstream culture. When activated, schemas are able to evaluate the new materials in light of previous knowledge.

37. **Answer: D. All of the above**
(Average) (Skill 5.6)
The language experience story followed good ESOL practice because background knowledge was activated, permitting more learning. As plants were part of the science curriculum, the story uses words from the content area, too. And, because the children wanted to communicate what they had learned, it represented real communication.

38. **Answer: D. realizes how Alicia's lack of exposure to English outside of the classroom is affecting her literacy development**
(Rigorous) (Skill 5.7)
By using data that has already been compiled, Ms. Rollman shows that she understands how important Alicia's educational history is, as well as, personal factors such as minimal exposure to English and the family's denial for bilingual services. Options A and C are not correct for this scenario as this knowledge is not derived from Alicia's data. Option B is not correct because using Alicia's data may not help Ms. Rollman select strategies for helping with sight word recognition.

39. **Answer: B. shows that she understands which instructional delivery practices are effective in developing ELLs' comprehension**
(Rigorous) (Skill 6.2)
Ms. Rollman shows that she understands the correct instructional strategies to use with ELLs, including graphic organizers, which present information in an organized and visual way. Graphic organizers help students place information in a comprehensible context. Options A and C are not correct as these strategies do not fall within the realm of cooperative learning or the use of graphic organizers. Option D will not support Alicia's comprehension and language development.

40. **Answer: A. focus on developing Alicia's phonological awareness of both her native language and the target language**
(Rigorous) (Skill 1.3)
By focusing on developing Alicia's phonological awareness of both languages, Ms. Rollman is helping Alicia with word recognitions skills and fluency while also helping to develop her cognitive capabilities. Since Alicia already has shown that she is reading on grade level in her native language, it is obvious that she is missing the basic foundations of the English language. Options B and C do not address the need to develop Alicia's reading comprehension. Rather fluency addresses the need to develop speaking skills. Option D is incorrect as developing basic phonological awareness takes precedence over sight word recognition, which is generally used for fluency.

41. Answer: C. Submersion with primary language support
(Average) (Skill 8.2)
Given Alicia's mastery of reading in her native language and her parent's approval for a bilingual setting, Option C is the best choice. Since the goal is English mastery, Alicia will be tutored or taught in her native language with the teachers using her first language to support English content classes. Structured English immersion uses little or no support in the native language. An ESL pull-out program would address not only her academic needs but also her social needs, and Alicia has given no indication of having trouble communicating with her peers. Option D describes her current classroom situation.

42. Answer: A. peer-mediated instruction
(Average) (Skill 6.1)
Peer-mediated instruction supports mastery of content, surpassing whole-class instruction, workbook activities, and question-answer sessions. By providing graphic organizers and a simplified rubric, Mr. Solis shows that he understands effective practices to engage students as well as the essential components of peer-mediated instruction. Option B and D are not strategies that are being used in this scenario. Option C is a strategy that matches pairs, or partners, in a tutoring situation with one student who has mastered a concept to one who still struggles.

43. Answer: B. students' strengths and weaknesses in the targeted objective
(Rigorous) (Skill 7.1)
Option B is the best answer because diagnosing strengths and weaknesses helps the instructor determine what else needs to be taught to students. Option A an example of a proficiency test, and Option C is an example of a norm-referenced test. Option D is incorrect as Mr. Solis is not preparing students for testing but rather, determining the direction for future lessons.

44. Answer: B. knows how to use ongoing assessments to plan and adjust instruction that addresses individual student needs, enabling students to achieve learning goals
(Rigorous) (Skill 7.6)
Mr. Alvera is using district assessment results to adjust his future instruction while helping students to create learning goals. Option A is incorrect as Mr. Alvera is not selecting or developing assessments. The other options are incorrect as these are district implemented tests for all students, not just for the ESL classroom, and they are not standardized tests.

45. Answer: A. The use of metacognition with students to help them recognize their thinking processes
(Average) (Skill 6.2)
The scenario states that Mr. Alvera meets with individual students to discuss their thinking processes while solving certain problems. Metacognition is when a student thinks about how he or she thinks while working through a learning

experience. It is an awareness of his or her thought processes. The other options are incorrect because there is no indication that the assessments are scaffolded in any way; no mention was made that these assessments are linguistically accommodating to students' level of English; and Mr. Alvera's purpose is not to develop academic language.

46. Answer: C. The personal factors that affect ELLs' content-area learning
(Rigorous) (Skill 6.4)
The best option is C because realizing an ELL's individual factors will help with his or her content-area learning. In this case the student has prior learning experiences and is competent in mathematical computation but is lacking in content vocabulary, which can hinder future success. Options A and B fail to specify what practices and resources Ms. Trinidad will use. Option D is incorrect because cultural differences are not a factor in this scenario.

47. Answer: D. Preteaching content vocabulary and helping the student apply familiar concepts to new learning experiences
(Rigorous) (Skill 6.2)
Both of these strategies acknowledge the student's academic needs and current level of concept knowledge. The student is competent in the subject but is lacking in the English vocabulary for the concepts. Option A is not correct as providing the written words does not help the student make connections between what is already known and what is being learned. Option B is incorrect as there is no mention of a need to provide intervention for critical thinking. Although both factors in Option C are necessary for the teacher to be aware of, the main focus is on helping the student make connections between what is already known and its new vocabulary.

48. Answer: B. Developing students' cognitive processes
(Rigorous) (Skill 6.3)
This particular strategy combines reasoning, perception, and intuition as students work through the problem using pictures to represent the gist of the problem. Option A is not correct because the activity is not to identify vocabulary but to incorporate reasoning with visual images. Option C is incorrect as this is not a group or partner activity. Option D is not correct as the goal of this activity is to make connections between what is known to the actual problem solving aspects of a problem.

49. Answer: A. TELPAS
(Average) (Skill 7.2)
Annually, every school-age ELL in the state of Texas takes the Texas English Language Proficiency Assessment System (TELPAS) test, which measures a child's English proficiency through listening, speaking, reading, and writing. The results are readily available to all educators who work with ELLs. The AAPPL is not used statewide in Texas for all ELLs but may be used by a district for initial academic placement. TOEFL is used to test college-age students and adults. The STAAR test does not test nor measure a child's level of English acquisition.

50. Answer: B. As a class, students say and mimic the words and actions of the P.E. teacher through each stage of the dance
(Rigorous) (Skill 8.4)
The teacher realized that using Total Physical Response (TPR) is the best process to use in order to determine and assess students' understanding of the movements. Option A is incorrect as not all ELLs are capable of competently reading in their original language. Plus, they may not make the connection between the words and the visual images. Option C is incorrect as placing students in smaller groups with more time does not guarantee that the majority of students will master the steps. Option D is not correct as the presence of a bilingual aide is not something that can be taken for granted and does not have the aide showing the movements as the aide describes them.

51. Answer: A. language proficiency
(Easy) (Skill 7.2)
Since the Test of English as a Foreign Language (TOEFL) tests a student's English language ability in reading comprehension, essay writing, syntax, and lexis, it tests for language proficiency.

52. Answer: C. Reviewing students' proficiency levels from previous TELPAS exams
(Rigorous) (Skill 7.3)
Option C is the correct answer because knowing the tests commonly used in ESL programs and interpreting the results of TELPAS will give the teacher a more definitive look at an ELL's progress from one year to the next. Options A, B, and D will not give the instructor a longitudinal look at students' past results with reading comprehension.

53. Answer: B. Intermediate
(Average) (Skill 7.3)
Julio's writing lacks details and contains numerous errors. Intermediate ELLs use incomplete or short, simple sentences, loosely connected texts, and parts of their writing may be hard to understand. It is clear that Julio has a limited ability to express ideas in writing. A beginning ELL lacks the English necessary to develop elements, such as focus, coherence, and the language structures necessary for understanding. Advanced ELLs have a grasp of basic verbs and tenses, and can construct complete sentences. Advanced-high ELLs have acquired English vocabulary and knowledge of structure to develop or demonstrate competency in writing.

54. Answer: C. Focus on simple and compound sentence structure using graphic organizers for writing organization with mini-lessons focusing on grammar usage
(Rigorous) (Skill 5.2)
It is obvious from the writing sample that Julio does not have a grasp of simple sentence structures, an indication that this is an intermediate student. The use of graphic organizers and mini-lessons on grammar usage will also support this student. Options A and B would be more appropriate for the advanced ELL. Option D would be appropriate for the advanced ELL who has a good grasp of the English language.

55. Answer: D. Jasmine's academic progress will be monitored for the next two years
(Average) (Skill 7.4)
Students who have been exited from an ESL program are to be monitored for two years. Options A, B, and C do not meet the guidelines that are the basis of the Language Proficiency Assessment Committee (LPAC).

56. Answer: D. Essay writing
(Average) (Skill 7.5)
Essay writing is not an appropriate strategy for evaluating the English capabilities of ELLs.

57. Answer: C. students were denied an "equal" education
(Rigorous) (Skill 8.1)
Option A refers to *Castaneda* v. *Pickard* (1981). Option B refers to Title IX of the Education Amendments of 1972. Option D was covered in Florida Educational Equity Act of 1984.

58. Answer: C. high-performing children cannot be used to average out low-performing ELLs
(Rigorous) (Skill 8.1)
The NCLB Act (2001) specifically states that disaggregated data must be used in evaluating school performance. Option A refers to the establishment of voluntary school participation in NAEP after the National Committee on Excellence in Education produced its report *A Nation at Risk* (1983). Option B refers to the decision rendered in *Castaneda* v. *Pickard* (1981). Option D refers to a requirement resulting from *Lau* v. *Nichols* (1974) that schools must form and convene assessment committees.

59. Answer: B. the community's value of the L2
(Average) (Skill 8.2)
Motivation is always a key factor in language learning, and when an ELL has community support for second language/cultural learning, bilingualism is greatly enhanced. Option B is the best option.

60. Answer: C. exposing the child to both languages as early as possible
(Average) (Skill 8.2)
Research on bilingualism suggests that children should be exposed to both languages from birth, when possible, for maximum bilingual benefit.

61. Answer: B. Available classrooms
(Average) (Skill 8.3)
Option B is the best factor for a district to consider when putting together an ELL program that is based on the pull-out model. Options A, C, and D are materials that would be found in any school and are not usually a factor to consider when implementing a program.

62. Answer: B. Speaking at a normal pace
(Average) (Skill 8.4)
Teachers must learn to slow their pace in order for ELLs to understand their speech. They should not, however, speak too slowly, nor raise their voice.

63. Answer: D. Increasing social contact with members of U.S. culture
(Rigorous) (Skill 9.1)
The amount of comprehensible input and output (linguistic variables) and the extent of connections with the new culture (sociocultural variables) affect language learning considerably. By developing new relationships with members of U.S. culture, ELLs are able to hear and use their new language in meaningful contexts in their daily lives, both of which are key elements in the development of L2.

64. Answer: A. Placing new students in the center or front of the classroom
(Average) (Skills 9.2, 9.3)
Option A is an excellent way to integrate ELLs into the mainstream of activities and to have them in a central position that helps to establish a sense of community. It reinforces a positive, effective learning environment. Option B does not directly impact the classroom environment. Option C is incorrect as materials foster language acquisition, not necessarily the overall classroom environment. Option D is not correct because celebrations address cultural diversities and are not an ongoing classroom activity.

65. Answer: D. Time
(Easy) (Skill 9.4)
In many cultures, time and its distinct manifestations (such as "being on time") is of little importance. Oftentimes, these students are allowed as much time as they need to finish a quiz or

assignment. Teaching time limitations on testing and class work may be a long, difficult process for ELLs from cultures where time is given so little consideration.

66. Answer: B. determine what they want to focus on for careers in their area
(Average) (Skill 9.5)
Option B provides students with a more global perspective on the benefits of being bilingual. Option A is not correct as the focus is upon the need for a second language, not selecting a career. Option C is not correct as the information being provided is more than just cultural organizations. Option D is incorrect as the materials do not directly address colleges and local community colleges.

67. Answer: D. Recommend the public library and its adult programs
(Easy) (Skill 10.1)
Suggesting programs about diet and exercise or sports would not be the best choices, unless the ESOL teacher is asked specifically about them. The public library would probably be the best choice for introducing adults to a world wider than the native-speaking community. Libraries have a variety of services that would serve many needs. Depending on the local facilities, libraries offer adult-education programs, book clubs for scholars, children's sections for harried parents, and computer classes.

68. Answer: A. knows how important it is to encourage participation of Spanish-speaking families in the school's activities
(Average) (Skill 10.2)
By bringing in volunteers, the ESL lead teacher is creating a language support that will encourage families to be a part of their child's education. Option B is not correct as the activity is not one that advocates for students but rather extends upon their learning and encourages family participation. Option C is not correct as there is no mention of resources being needed or used. Option D is incorrect as the ESL lead teacher did not mention a concern about adult participation.

69. Answer: D. Simple board games incorporating ESOL techniques
(Easy) (Skill 10.3)
Options A, B, and C are all traditional activities for interesting families in their children's school.

Option D would offer the grandparents the opportunity to read and ask questions about the ESOL program of their grandchildren. Remember, TESOL (in all its distinct forms—ESL, EFL, EAP, ESOL—in addition to TESOL) has changed tremendously since the days of grammar translation, which may be the only form of language learning the grandparents are familiar with.

70. Answer: B. Permit children who immigrated to the U.S. at an early age to acquire legal status independently of their parents
(Average) (Skill 10.4)
The DREAM Act has had its ups and downs, but it promises to legalize children who, through no fault of their own, are being raised in another country, though it may be the only home they have known. The act would apply only to minors who are of good moral character, and under certain other conditions.

CPSIA information can be obtained at www.ICGtesting.com
Printed in the USA
LVOW09s2359150616

492806LV00019B/111/P